SKYLINES HONG KONG

SKYLINES Hong Kong
©FormAsia Books Limited

Published by: FormAsia Books Limited
Suite 706
Yu Yuet Lai Building
45 Wyndham Street
Central. Hong Kong
ISBN: 962-7283-26-6

Written by: Peter Moss
Designed by: Robert Hookham
Illustrated by: Ian Leung
Produced by: Format Limited
Proofread by: Peter Thomas
Text/Photography © FormAsia Books Limited
Editorial Assistance: Deepa Nand, Mike Tanner,
Heinz Rüst, Dr Patrick Hase, Keith Kerr, Gordon Ongly,
Patrick Bruce, Philip Bruce. Edward Roblin

Printed in Hong Kong by: Hong Kong Prime Printing Co Ltd
Colour separations by: Sky Art Graphic Company Limited

SKYLINES
HONG KONG

Peter Moss

FormAsia

CONTENTS

INTRODUCTION

Architecture is a visual language that speaks for any city and those who live in it, serving as a symbolic expression of a people's aspirations, values and identity.

The introduction into Hong Kong of western-style architecture, more than 150 years ago, was the inevitable adjunct of British colonialism planted here in 1842. But its advent transformed the appearance of the Hong Kong skyline almost as dramatically as the even greater and more rapid metamorphosis that was to follow when Shanghai became the orient's greatest trading entrepôt of its time.

It was Hong Kong that paved the way, sustaining the initial impact of the west's assault on eastern sensibilities, and it was Hong Kong that continued smelting the mettles of both traditions to forge the shape and style in which this especially restless city has emerged.

The ever changing *mise-en-scene* of the Hong Kong skyline testifies to the vigour of the quickening currents that merged here to fashion its singular character. The pace at first was slow, the economy *laissez-faire,* the labour a constant supply of immigrants from mainland China, many of them treating Hong Kong as a temporary foothold from which to launch their excursions further afield. Hong Kong was a city of transients, living in a 'borrowed place' and on 'borrowed time'.

The area known as Central, or the City of Victoria as it used to be called, represented then, as it does now, the heart of urban Hong Kong. The architecture here today may look utterly different from the solemn civic grandeur it has usurped. But its essential role is no different to what it was at the outset. Its purpose remains unchanged, the intention being to embody and exemplify wealth and power.

What looks nostalgically appealing in old photographs of three to four storeyed Neo-classical Victorian structures, fronted by arcades and verandahs along the waterfront, comprised no more than typical

office block developments erected by the commercially-minded developers of their day.

Blessed with the surviving spirit of that *laissez-faire* philosophy still prevalent here, we have never been limited in choice, never been subjected to a single-style architecture dominating our skyline. Since Victorian times, our architecture has been labelled a 'hodge-podge', and this label still applies. Our commercially minded society has little appetite for grandiose civic centres or dignified edifices, public or private, designed by renowned architects.

The one conspicuous exception to this rule was the Hong Kong Bank, which aimed to impress by sheer pomp and circumstance when it invested large sums of money in the first two of its three successive headquarters in 1886 and 1935. But where their successor, in 1985, was intended to achieve the same impact, it confounded all expectations by markedly departing from the sober spirit of its predecessors and flaunting an entirely novel matrix through which it exposed its sheer technological supremacy.

I look upon this heterogeneous mixture of architecture in a positive way because we in Hong Kong have been spared that straitjacket of 'national style'. Each building, whether dressed in skin-deep curtain walls or adorned with post-modern embellishments, whether seeming anonymous, ambiguous, or embarrassingly out of place, is a statement in itself. It may not so much conform to its environment as declare its separation from it, but collectively these individual statements, set against green hills and blue waters, have given Hong Kong an unmistakable character all its own.

Such commercially driven societal force has produced a distinctive culture. The resulting flexibility, or spiritual freedom, generates opportunities, choice and change. Hong Kong is a city of paradox and it is through its *yin-yang* dynamics that we find our way forward. Our architecture reflects this reality.

STORMING
THE HEIGHTS

Hong Kong is a concentration – of place, people, energy
and intellect.

The constraints defining how this city would grow were
compounded of history and circumstance, scarcity of land and
declivity of terrain. Between them they shaped what is arguably
the world's most outstanding example of an architectural matrix
evolving from the special needs of its inhabitants.

But those same constraints also fashioned a metropolis that
betrays little of its origins, for in its restless desire to extract the
utmost from available resources, Hong Kong has obliterated
virtually all trace of where it began less than two centuries ago.

Distinctive of its approach to accommodating some of the
planet's highest population densities is the layered profile of
Hong Kong's urban development. Overlaying strata of
transportation routes, pedestrian walkways, shopping arcades and
public gardens are stacked one above the other to provide vertical
rather than horizontal access.

Location – that keyword beloved of all realtors – was, from the
outset, the prime consideration. Everything had to be shoehorned
into one small island on the South China coast, its topography so
vertiginous that when it embarked on its astonishing career in
1842, the embryonic trading settlement was compelled to align
itself along a narrow strip of foreshore fronting the harbour that
had summoned it into existence. It became a city that lived by,
for and because of the sea.

The first of many reclamations from that sea was undertaken
within nine years of the city's foundation, setting the pattern for
subsequent extensions of the shoreline out into the harbour
which, by the time of the Japanese invasion in 1941 – a hundred
years after Hong Kong's inception – had added one thousand
four hundred and twenty-five acres, or more than two square
miles, to the total land mass. Even by conservative calculations,
such accretions to both the original island, its adjoining land
mass and the even larger neighbouring island of Lantau, have
since multiplied that figure tenfold.

But insufficiency of usable building land was not the only factor
predicating either this recourse to artificial supplement or the
perpendicular thrust of the structural forms that absorbed its
availability as soon as it was created. Still more compelling was
the urgent dictate of public demand.

The first prerequisite, of even the earliest of the many waves of
immigrants who began flooding into Hong Kong from the China
mainland, was proximity of home to place of employment.
Because an unhindered capacity to work presented the fastest and

surest route to economic salvation, the new arrivals would prefer to waste as little time as possible in transit between the two.

If they could not actually reside at the workplace itself they would choose to live directly above, as was the case with the pioneer shophouses crowding the heights above Western District and Kennedy Town.

This willing sacrifice of comfort and seclusion, to the demands of convenience and accessibility, suggested a solution first posed within the government's public works department, who were charged with the mammoth task of creating vast rehousing schemes, and eventually whole new townships, into which could be decanted the tremendous influx of new arrivals in the post-war years.

Resettlement became the rallying cry of an administration driven to the wall by the problems of coping with thousands upon thousands of refugees, who crowded into perilous and vulnerable squatter areas ascending the hillsides, where they were prone to flood and fire, rainstorm and landslide.

Private developers took their cue from the multi-dimensional array initially devised as an expedient to meet pressures of circumstance. If it served to make life more convenient in low-cost public housing estates, there was no reason why it should not prove equally applicable to more sophisticated residential and commercial environments.

They set out to improve upon the all-in-one formula that packaged homes, offices, commercial precincts, service utilities and transportation nodes into one irresistibly convenient parcel. Integrated estates, equivalent to fair-sized townships elsewhere in the world, became the building blocks of new satellite cities spreading out into the rural hinterlands beyond the Kowloon foothills.

The rapid growth of the Mass Transit Railway in the eighties, with accompanying development rights over station complexes, spread its own nexus of expansion, planting tendrils like some rampantly territorial efflorescence through established urban areas and beyond.

The rest of the world, confounded by the evidence that it *was* possible to compact human populations within hitherto inconceivable spatial limitations, came to observe, admire and, where feasible, imitate. Hong Kong palpably dispelled nightmarish visions of urban proliferation portrayed in Fritz Lang's 1926 cinematic masterpiece "Metropolis", prompting the Deutsches Architektur-Museum in Frankfurt to mount a special exhibition in 1993/94, entitled "Hong Kong Architecture – the Aesthetics of Density".

9

Chroniclers of the Hong Kong skyline date back to the late nineteenth century. In each account one detects an eye for the natural amphitheatre which set the stage for a striking synthesis between architecture and environment; that dramatic combination of harbour and encircling mountains that created one of the world's most instantly recognizable panoramas.

Some visitors, lost for parallels, fell back on those that could be called to mind, however inappropriate. Not a few likened Hong Kong to Gibraltar, if for no other reason than the fact that the two shared the same distinctive bulwark of mountain overshadowing man's efforts to subdue it into some form of harmonious coexistence. In Hong Kong's case, as time has shown, that subjugation was to prove infinitely more successful.

Its mountainous backdrop delineates both Hong Kong's character and its frame of reference. The steady ascent of its lower slopes, in serried ranks of building upon building, each successively replaced many times throughout Hong Kong's relatively brief history, constitutes the symmetry for which this city is best remembered.

There is, however, an obverse side to the coin. By using its mountains as yardsticks on which to peg its ambitions, Hong Kong has risked forfeiting the principal component of its inimitable appearance.

Viewed now from the sea, or from the opposite shores of Kowloon, it seems so intent on storming the heights that the sheer scale and mass of its endeavours all but obscures the view. The result is a triumph of architecture over environment perhaps, but a loss of the felicitous balance that once brought out the best of both.

Those in love with the past, or seeking a continuity of architectural expression whose roots can be logically traced back through time, will be largely disappointed in Hong Kong, where buildings of any antiquity are sometimes more valued for their scarcity than for any intrinsic architectural merit.

Those beguiled by the future, and in particular by the advent of the third millennium, will be fascinated to discover a city in ferment, endlessly reworking and reshaping itself, going back over the same ground again and again to maximize its potential.

Cramming more floor space within a given plot ratio, to obtain the best returns and achieve the most striking visual effect the site will allow, is an objective too often assayed simply by striving to be bigger, better and more imposing than the competition.

10

The cumulative effect is of a city obsessed with sheer scale; caught up in a race the west has long abandoned, but with which the east still seems excessively preoccupied. Quiet respectability becomes less important than ostentatious braggadocio and sheer verve, producing results which – whether triumphant success or spectacular failure – will not escape attention.

The challenge afforded by each new commission has been a boon to the development of Hong Kong's resident architectural expertise. Trained overseas, most young architects have returned steeped in western traditions, setting out to demonstrate they are capable of matching the best that can be produced by leading practitioners from abroad. What they have so far failed to achieve is an evolution of indigenous forms that would offer the first glimmerings of an authentically "Hong Kong" style.

With too few exceptions, they submit to preconceived notions of clients content to compete with, rather than depart from, the edifices erected by their rivals. While architects look for opportunities to boldly go where none have gone before, big business prefers to stick with the proven and reliable. The spirit of adventure is less entrenched in Hong Kong's commercial bastions than is a belief in established formulae and popular taste.

Whatever may account for this neglect, Hong Kong appears to have turned its back on the last concrete evidence of its history, as expressed through the fabric with which that history was associated. Its traces have largely disappeared, and with them have gone all strands of a definable evolutionary trend that might have bridged past and present as a platform on which to found the future.

Few vestiges remain of the colonial heritage which, for more than a century and a half, until Hong Kong's reversion to Chinese sovereignty in 1997, channeled and energized its volatile progress. Were it not for the former Supreme Court building that now houses the seat of its legislature, and an abandoned Government House reduced to the status more of a mausoleum than museum, Hong Kong would already be bereft of intelligible clues to account for its apparent eruption into the twenty-first century, as though it were born but yesterday.

The Antiquities and Monuments Board has dedicated itself to the salvation of whatever historical buildings it can snatch from the jaws of excavators and the hammers of demolition crews. But much has so far escaped its ambit. Unless these limited achievements are reinforced, Hong Kong stands in danger of appearing a society so zealously absorbed in the future that it has consciously expunged its memories, seemingly content to inhabit a city without a past.

KOWLOON CANTON CLOCK TOWER

Tsim Sha Tsui, Kowloon

Like a solitary arm raised in protest against unrelenting eradication of the past, the Kowloon Canton Clock Tower stands as sole remnant of a rail terminus where it was once possible to purchase a ticket for the world's longest overland odyssey. Inaugurated in 1910, the Kowloon Canton Railway represented the first stage of a link that would transport the traveller to Beijing and thence, on the Trans-Siberian Railway across the steppes of Russia, to Moscow for connection with onward European destinations.

Never a conspicuously imposing building, when compared with the opulence of terminals designed to express grander imperial aspirations, the Kowloon Canton station was nevertheless so strategically located, as the dot on the apostrophe of the Kowloon peninsula, that it topped the list of the world's most convenient and accessible points of embarkation. One had only to walk a few yards from the Star Ferry terminus, or from Kowloon wharves disembarking sea voyagers, to board a train that would bear one on a picnic excursion to the New Territories, or on a long spell of home leave after years of toiling in a disagreeable climate.

And here, at the advent of every lunar new year, thousands of Chinese would swamp the platforms, encumbered with gifts for their relatives in southern China.

All of this hubbub and excitement was stilled overnight when the KCR completed a comprehensive modernization programme to double-track its entire route, replace diesel locomotives with high-speed electrified trains, and relocate its terminus to newly reclaimed land in Tsim Sha Tsui East. An impassioned campaign by conservationists, including a petition that amassed thousands of signatures, failed to avert demolition of the original terminal building, whose site is now occupied by a controversially windowless cultural complex, leaving only this amputated clock tower to mourn its passing.

HONG KONG PARK CONSERVATORY

Cotton Tree Drive, Central

Asked to design an indoor games hall, together with miscellaneous installations scattered through a green enclave that once housed a military barracks in the heart of the city, Edward Ho of Wong Tung & Partners Limited, persuaded the Urban Council that the whole area would benefit from an integrated plan. He had two choices: to return it to an entirely natural domain, interlaced with footpaths, or make use of the various interesting platforms left behind by the demolished army quarters. The latter, he thought, could be blended into surviving vegetation as pediments for a variety of amenities of far greater interest and attraction to the general public.

Unveiled in 1991, the ten-hectare park has provided much needed green lungs in the heart of the city, affording a series of terraced delights from a visual arts centre, utilizing one of the surviving barracks, to a children's playground and giant walk-through aviary, where one views birds from treetop height on an elevated wooden path. The aviary is overlooked by a tai chi garden and lookout tower, below which is a circular outdoor theatre of classical Graecian proportions, adjoining a massive conservatory (opposite) whose interlocking rooms, sunlit through a stepped pyramid of glass, sequester varieties of plants in different temperature and humidity zones. Beyond is a waterfall, whose intricate synthetic rock formation would be at home on an antique Chinese scroll, descending beside a restaurant with an alfresco dining courtyard.

At the coiled heart of this constellation lies an artificial lake, ringed by trees which frame superb perspectives of surrounding skylines. The public would seem to agree with architect Ho when he confesses that the lake is his favourite feature. The considerable pedestrian traffic traversing this park, between Central's commercial centre and the busy precincts of Pacific Place, momentarily slows here to absorb the effects of nature cajoled by man into a happy union with his artifice.

GOVERNMENT HOUSE

Upper Albert Road, Central

Queen Victoria's earliest representatives in Hong Kong were viewed as an encumbrance the mercantile community must suffer in order to qualify for protection under her flag. While the homes of affluent taipans reflected increasing wealth and status, the first three governors, Pottinger (1841-44), Davis (1844-48) and Bonham (1848-54), rented the best accommodation their relatively meagre stipends could support.

Only at the close of Bonham's tenure, too late for him to avail himself of its completion, was work commenced on a permanent gubernatorial residence. Surveyor General Charles Cleverly came up with a plan costing fourteen thousand nine hundred and forty pounds, roughly within London's estimate. Bowring became the building's first occupant and, within days of moving in, was sobered by the inauspicious collapse of a mast in the process of erection on his front lawn, killing a workman and seriously injuring two others.

Later incumbents have been known to consult geomancers in their endeavours to avert ill fortune, particularly in the closing years of colonial realm when Government House began to sink, like a faltering ship of state, into its protective greenery, far below the palisades of high-rise towers that deprived it of its once magisterial prospect of harbour and Kowloon hills. A cutting edge of the new Bank of China Tower, in particular, was deemed by feng shui experts to require particular remedial measures through strategic locations of defensive shrubbery.

In all twenty-five governors, from Bowring onwards, together with two Japanese lieutenant generals, have occupied Government House through its various expansions and accretions, the most efficacious of which was instigated by Lieutenant General Rensuke Isogai, who commissioned Seichi Fujimura to remodel the building. This young architect's single most striking embellishment is an unmistakably Japanese tower that provides the structure's focal point and imparts symmetry to what had previously been an arbitrary architectural accumulation.

ST JOHN'S CATHEDRAL
4-8 Garden Road, Central

Occupying the only freehold land in Hong Kong, St John's Anglican Cathedral is one of the few structures to survive the frenzy of construction that took place in Hong Kong's first decade as a colony of the British crown; much evidence of which was quickly erased by catastrophic typhoons and by a restless desire to build afresh.

Inaugurated in 1849, the cathedral's only predecessor from that period is Flagstaff House (1846), now the Tea Museum in Hong Kong Park. London architect Hardwick envisaged St John's in Gothic Revival mode, but later adapted the design to conform with the empire style popular with churches of the Victorian era. Considerable modifications were necessitated by a reduced budget and limitations of local workmanship. The total bill for construction was eight thousand seven hundred and thirty-six pounds. The tower was added in 1850 and the chancel substantially expanded in 1873.

The cathedral suffered the humiliation of being turned into a social club by Japanese occupation forces during World War II, when the tower was pierced by a shell and it lost its stained glass windows, polished altars and choir stalls. Since its restoration, it has steadily become a church of the people, rather than the privileged assembly of Hong Kong's elite it had previously tended to be.

On 11 March 1997 celebrations led by the Dean of St John's, The very Reverend Philips, marked the one hundred and fiftieth anniversary of that day when, for the first time, pioneer settlers of Hong Kong gathered for worship under a solid roof instead of a temporary matshed.

Where once it overlooked a military parade ground symbolizing the panoply of imperial power, today it stands as a quiet retreat in a green oasis at Hong Kong's heart, straddling the seat of government and the fount of commerce.

CITIBANK PLAZA

3 Garden Road, Central

Arms outstretched to embrace approaching visitors,
Citibank Plaza exemplifies architect Rocco Yim's philosophy
that a conjoined development of this stature should draw upon
its surroundings as an integral component of its design
rationale. Because the ground floor was volunteered as a
permanent right of way, keeping it accessible to the public
around the clock, the plaza gained a bonus increment to its
plot ratio.

Yim aimed to balance the adjacent Bank of China's sharply
angular contours with an L-shaped plan, linking a double
parallelogram to a curvilinear façade that resembles a
reflective shield. Between these asymmetrical wings,
"in keeping with Hong Kong's spontaneity and freedom from
rigid constraints", a flight of stairs ascends through the main
portico to the soaring ground floor lobby, which affords easy
access to the interior retail and club facilities, to neighbouring
buildings further along the Garden Road incline and across a
footbridge to the green refuge of Hong Kong Park.

While later rivals have followed its lead, Citibank Plaza was
the first privately developed commercial building to
incorporate such features as raised floors and an optic-fibre
telecommunications "backbone". Altogether its achievement
is a far cry from its predecessor on this site, a utilitarian
two-storey government block reputed to have been used,
during World War II, as an interrogation centre by the
Japanese Imperial Army.

BANK OF CHINA TOWER

1 Garden Road, Central

Introducing his design for the new Bank of China headquarters in Hong Kong, I.M. Pei described the commission as one that held considerable emotional appeal. His father was the bank's first Hong Kong manager of the Nationalist era. "You can't expect strong traditional Chinese elements," he cautioned. "I didn't design a pagoda." The only recognizably Chinese aspect in what he proposed was a two-ton granite base, reminiscent of Beijing's ancient city gates. From that rose a towering monolith of almost crystalline jaggedness, its huge, interlocking triangular surfaces tapering through a series of indentations around a central spine, to a slim bladed spire supporting two antennae that thrust well beyond its seventy storeys to a height of three hundred and fifteen metres, making it the tallest building in Hong Kong.

The result elicited admiration from those excited by innovative and aesthetically pleasing design, and consternation from those who saw it as a major disruption to the feng shui of its surroundings. Based on ancient precepts of harmony with nature, feng shui (literally meaning wind and water) abhors angles which, according to geomancer Sung Siu-kwong, "are like knives aimed at one." Two of the angles pointed at Government House and the Legislative Council chambers. Pei countered that "Geometric precision yields sharp edges," and confided that the design had been inspired by a bamboo sapling, seen by Chinese as a symbol of strength and endurance.

A rush to complete construction by 8 August 1988, regarded as the century's most auspicious date as the numeral eight in Cantonese sounds akin to the word for prosperity, failed to meet its objective, so that the bank had to settle instead for a topping out ceremony on that day. Later a series of pools and waterfalls, descending through the bank's terraced garden surrounds, added their own feng shui enhancement because, as Pei pointed out, "Water is an auspicious and restorative force."

CHEUNG KONG
CENTER

2 Queen's Road Central

Standing seventy storeys tall in the heart of Central District, Cheung Kong Center rises in a perfectly symmetrical square, almost as an antithesis to the sharp, angular lines of the adjoining Bank of China Tower on the opposite side of Garden Road. Despite the fact that the bank preceded it by some ten years, this juxtaposition has prompted some to describe it as the box in which the bank was shipped.

Eschewing poetry in favour of pragmatism, Cheung Kong Center packs within its blandly utilitarian curtain wall of silver reflective glazing some of the biggest surprises in Hong Kong's architectural scene, including totally integrated and computerized lighting circuitry that can transform its façades into giant illuminated display panels configured to any design. Concept architect for this exterior was Cesar Pelli, working with Leo Daly for Hsin Yieh Architects & Associates.

It also offers some of the most commodious and sensibly planned office accommodation in Hong Kong, elevated on raised floors to allow for convenient ducting of utilities, including air-conditioning, and equipped with fan powered terminal units which can be moved to permit maximum temperature control. Twenty-eight passenger lifts serve the building from the ground and upper ground floor lobbies. Rising at nine metres per second, these display up-to-the-minute news and worldwide stock market information.

Offset at an angle, which emphasizes its distinction from neighbouring buildings, the Cheung Kong Center has contributed to the variety of contrasting styles that serves to make this area of Central of particular architectural interest. Located on a site formerly occupied by the Hilton Hotel, the development provides for extensive landscaping, including a large waterfall, all of which opens up attractive vistas of ancient banyan trees, palms and veteran neighbouring buildings; among them St John's Cathedral (1849) and the Court of Final Appeal, housed in the red-bricked French Mission Building (1911).

MURRAY BUILDING

Garden Road, Central

The Architectural Services Department is generally viewed by Hong Kong's wider architectural profession in much the same light as artists view artisans. It is seen as competent, predictably reliable and wholly uninspired. Major civic buildings designed by civil servants arouse misgivings similar to those that might attend a signboard painter unleashed on the ceiling of the Sistine Chapel. The bigger the assignment, the greater the apprehension. Witness the controversy unleashed when the government employed its architects to develop a new Cultural Centre on the Tsim Sha Tsui waterfront. The result was roundly condemned for resembling a ski-jump and failing to take advantage of one of the world's finest harbour views.

It came as a pleasant surprise, therefore, when the department unveiled its own offices in Murray Building, which has since been home to a succession of other government tenants. Architects Bill Shewan and Colin Bramwell had come up with an innovative departure from accepted practice by recessing windows at a forty-five degree angle, so as to conserve energy by filtering sunlight. Effectively they had produced Hong Kong's first environmentally efficient building.

However, the best laid plans of civil servants oft run aground on the reefs of public accountants, who make no allowance for trimmings that might lift the extraordinary into the realms of the superb. It was their misfortune to work under the eagle eye of a financial secretary who, having been assured that the building's distinguishing design feature would reduce glare, decreed there would be no provision for standard issue venetian blinds.

While they performed excellently on the structure's other façades, the recessed windows failed to fulfill expectations on the eastern face. Civil servants on that side put up a united front of cardboard and newspaper screens, generally disfiguring the building's geometrically clean contours. When motorists along Cotton Tree Drive, who included the élite of Hong Kong's Peak dwellers, pointed fingers in disbelief, the requisite blinds were granted.

BANK OF CHINA

1 Bank Street, Central

Completion of the Bank of China in 1950 followed shortly after the Communist party came to power on the mainland, and therefore marked a celebration befitting the historical importance of that event. It was no accident that the bank should choose, as its architects, the very firm that had designed the neighbouring HongkongBank when that bastion came to prominence in 1935.

Palmer and Turner, whose own history is linked with some of the oldest and most redoubtable buildings in Hong Kong and Shanghai, were commissioned to ensure that the Bank of China surpassed its rival in height, while emulating the stolid, granite faced respectability that building had unmistakably achieved. Even the HongkongBank's familiar lions were to have their Chinese counterparts fronting the new structure.

A massive vault door, ordered from the United States, was never delivered because of the introduction of a United Nations embargo on trade with China, following that country's entry into the Korean War. Legend has it that the door still sits in some North American warehouse, gathering dust.

When Hong Kong was subjected to an overspill of the Cultural Revolution in 1967, the Bank of China bristled with loudspeakers inciting revolution against the colonial authorities.

Such political divergence seems remote from the venerable appearance this structure now presents under its present tenants, the Sin Hua Bank. Its role in the heart of the city has been further enhanced by the imaginative China Club, occupying the upper floors and uniting East and West in the convivial atmosphere of prewar Shanghai.

Never did the bank play so focal a role as in 1976, which saw the death of China's two revered leaders, Chairman Mao Zedong and Head of State Zhou Enlai. The queues quietly waiting to pay their respects wound through several blocks of Central.

THE HONGKONG AND SHANGHAI BANKING CORPORATION LIMITED

1 Queen's Road Central

If money were the religion of Hong Kong, "the Bank" would be its cathedral. Until Norman Foster's revolutionary design for the headquarters of The Hongkong and Shanghai Banking Corporation, the public image of this edifice, as exemplified by all three predecessors on its fundamentally strategic site, was of an inscrutable, granite-faced fortress, safeguarding the community's financial stability.

Foster, recently awarded his profession's top honour with the coveted Pritzker Prize, triggered consternation when he abandoned the premise that a bank must be a bastion. He postulated, instead, that it should show a transparently open, public face, placing itself at the service of the customer as a conveniently accessible and user-friendly resource which inspired affection rather than awed reverence. Nervous eyes were fixed upon the outcome, for the site he worked with held almost spiritual significance in the geomantic atlas determining Hong Kong's fortunes, straddling the principal artery through which dragon's blood flowed from The Peak, through Government House and out into the harbour. Interference with that feng shui force line would place the entire population in jeopardy. The superstitious solemnly noted that Hong Kong's confidence waned with the demolition of the old building in the early eighties, and was restored only when its successor was declared open in 1986.

In place of the craggy monolith that stood here since its own ceremonial inauguration in 1935, there now rises a high-tech marvel of steel masts supporting a series of diagonal trusses, each two storeys deep and suspending floors like trays on a giant tea trolley, whose unobstructed interiors are drenched in natural light. Equally unobstructed is the flow of pedestrian traffic at ground level, which provides an open public thoroughfare at any hour of the day or night. Twin escalators, curiously angled to conform with the directions of geomancers, transport customers into a vast central atrium, eleven levels deep, which despite its unmistakably modernist attributes is curiously reminiscent of some high gothic paean to a mediaeval faith.

THE HONG KONG CLUB

1 Jackson Road, Central

The need of a well defined social pecking order, and an exchange for gossip and intrigue, drove Hong Kong's pioneer expatriate community to rate the establishment of a club as one of its earliest priorities. Here, traders could seek refuge from wives, public servants could engage in wary fraternisation with the private sector and all members could indulge their cordial dislike of whoever happened to be the current incumbent at Government House. The delicate task of determining who should be admitted was alleviated by the pleasure of turning down those who would not.

Founded in 1844, the club was first situated in Wyndham Street, its colonnaded, three-storey façade fronting an avenue of trees that shaded sedan chair bearers patiently awaiting the exodus of frequently inebriated "fares". In 1897 the premises were removed to a more imposing, four-storey clubhouse located on newly reclaimed waterfront, whose awninged balconies gazed disdainfully down on the less privileged passing its august precincts in Club Road.

An extraordinary general meeting in 1980 saw membership divided on the question of whether to preserve or demolish that venerable building. The pro-demolitionists won and Australian architect Harry Seidler was awarded the design for the new clubhouse. Respect for the dignity of Cenotaph Square, which the new building would overlook, prompted Seidler to opt for subtly fluent curves that echoed something of the baroque style of the original. The emphasis of the building became inward looking, as if turning away from traffic noise infinitely greater than in the days of horse carriages and rickshaws. Light from the rotunda permeated all the main club floors, contributing to a sense of space largely unrestrained by columns and other supporting structures. Opening its doors in 1985, the new club preserved an aura of refuge from the travails of what had, since the inception of the original more than one hundred and forty years earlier, become one of the world's most stressful cities.

THE LEGISLATIVE COUNCIL BUILDING

8 Jackson Road, Central

When Victoria has ceased to be a city, when the harbour has silted up, when even the Hong Kong Club has crumbled away, this building will remain like a pyramid to commemorate the genius of the Far East. So foretold Chief Justice Sir Francis Piggott, accepting the key to the Supreme Court from Governor Sir Frederick Lugard, at its inaugural ceremony on 15 January 1912. Although his prophecy awaits fulfilment, the structure itself has undergone considerable modification, for on 30 October 1985 it was officially reopened as home of Hong Kong's Legislative Council.

In his inaugural address, Lugard complained that "these courts of justice have taken long to build and cost much money." The contract for the foundations on newly reclaimed harbour frontage had been let twelve years earlier, and the foundation stone laid on 12 November 1903. The building contractor, Chan Ah-tong, had died in the course of construction, to be replaced by his son.

Progress was hindered by a shortage of suitable granite, quarried on Stonecutters Island, and of trained stonemasons to work it. Architects Aston Webb and E. Ingress Bell, responsible for some of London's finest architecture, including Admiralty Arch, the Victoria and Albert Museum and the façade of Buckingham Palace, departed from their brief by orienting the building to face east, towards the former cricket grounds, now Chater Gardens, rather than west towards Statue Square. They argued that to rotate it would necessitate redesigning the interior, which proved not to be the case when it was eventually turned on its axis to conform with the initial specification.

Still surmounted by a statue of Blind Justice, this conspicuous heirloom of high colonial grandeur remains enshrined as seat of Hong Kong's legislature, its arcaded galleries overlooking an arena where once was enacted the pomp and circumstance of empire, and where today citizens still assemble, when occasion warrents, to exercise their freedom of expression.

MANDARIN ORIENTAL

5 Connaught Road Central

Working long hours to map the layout of the Mandarin Oriental hotel, John Howorth, of Leigh and Orange, suffered a near fatal accident. Returning late at night to his home above the Sha Tin valley, he crossed the harbour on the vehicular ferry - then the only means of doing so - and made the mistake of turning left instead of right when he descended the exit ramp at Jordan Road. The car sank rapidly, with Howorth struggling to release himself before it disappeared underwater. Assisting Howorth in the project was Frank Eckerman, who later took over the final stages. Their structure replaced Queen's Building, also designed by Leigh and Orange back in 1902.

Originally intended to serve as an office block, the new building was to retain the name of its progenitor, so that subsequent evolution into a hotel, back in 1961, would have produced the Queen's Hotel. Instead it opened its doors in 1963 as the Mandarin Hotel.

Hamish Cowperthwaite took over from original interior designer Don Ashton the task of easing this much-loved establishment through subtle transformations, over a span of years, that saw bars and restaurants come and go while the lobby retained much of its original flavour. Gold bas-reliefs encrusting the lobby walls were originally purchased by an avid American collector, whose plans to send them home to the States were frustrated by a UN embargo on trade with China. Other long-time favourites like the Chinnery Bar, with reproductions of paintings by renowned China coast artist George Chinnery, have been extensively remodelled. Until the late 80's the Chinnery was a male preserve.

One of Cowperthwaite's most remarkable restorations was the rooftop swimming pool, long buried under the former Harbour Room, which he revived in the style of a Roman bath. Where it once overlooked panoramic vistas of sea and mountains, the hotel is now more noticeably inward looking, a jewel box savoured by those with the key to unlock such delights as the Mandarin Grill, the Captain's Bar, Clipper Lounge and the Man Wah Chinese restaurant.

ENTERTAINMENT BUILDING

40 Queen's Road Central

Queen's Road Central has come a long way since its origins as the waterfront of Hong Kong's earliest settlement just over a century and a half ago. But its canyons of glass, steel and concrete are arrestingly relieved at the point – between its intersections with Wyndham and Stanley streets – where the old King's Theatre once lured cinema goers in the days before television and other forms of instant electronic gratification.

There, under the beguilingly deceptive but now totally inappropriate name of the Entertainment Building, architect Remo Riva of Palmer and Turner, was commissioned by classical devotees Thomas and Joseph Lau of Evergo, to design a building that would be not so much a throwback to the past as a successor to its fine traditions of craftsmanship and detail. His concept has achieved that objective in a way which singles it out from everything else in its vicinity.

Finished in a shade of beige granite that can only be found in Brazil, the structure is turned forty-five degrees from its original axis to open up triangular plazas, with a great deal more daylight at street level, and to afford tenants of its twenty-eight floors of office space more interesting views than they would otherwise be subjected to in the customary head-on configuration with adjoining buildings.

Perhaps the tower's most distinctive feature is the flat panel at the rear, which contains the service core, including lifts and stairwells, but also screens it from quaint but less visually appealing prospects over Lan Kwai Fong towards the terraced heights of Mid-Levels. Riva enjoyed the opportunity to incorporate the kind of felicitous touches lacking in too many contemporary styles. In particular, he sought to relieve the building's vertical geometry with curvilinear embellishments, in the forms of arches at podium level and balconies projecting like the edges of a giant discus at the twenty-eighth floor.

BANK OF EAST ASIA

10 Des Voeux Road Central

A rare example of a Hong Kong building looking over its shoulder to its antecedents, the Bank of East Asia, when it opened in its current manifestation in 1978, incorporated elements of its predecessor, which had also been designed by Palmer and Turner in the early years of the twentieth century. Among these souvenirs were flagpoles supported by griffins and, mounted on a wall overlooking the main banking hall, the vault door of the original bank. Also dramatically featured in the main hall are four large paintings of spring, summer, autumn and winter in Chinese ink and colour by Kan Tai-keung and, in wooden relief, a sculpture by Cheung Yee depicting one hundred forms of the Chinese character for happiness and fortune.

Conceived by Remo Riva to complement neighbouring developments of that period, including The Landmark and Alexandra House, the bank is finished in a cladding of dark grey granite, chosen by its owners to provide a contrast with its surroundings. Offices of the chairman and executives are located at the top of the building, accessed via a service core aligned along its eastern side to allow maximum floor space on each level.

The Bank of East Asia serves as a quiet reminder, in the heart of the city, of the dignity one has been accustomed to expect of a bank. From this modestly restrained hub spreads a banking empire that incorporates seventeen outlets in China, a regional network in Singapore, Vietnam, Malaysia and the Philippines, and a global network extending to the USA, UK, Canada and the British Virgin Islands. An integral part of Hong Kong's skyline from its inception on 4 January 1919, the bank recently commemorated eighty years of service that have entrenched its role as the world's largest independent Chinese bank.

東亞銀行
THE BANK OF EAST ASIA

JARDINE HOUSE

1 Connaught Place, Central

When it rose from reclaimed land in 1973, to attain new heights on the Hong Kong skyline, Jardine House – then known as Connaught Centre – effectively qualified as Hong Kong's first true "skyscraper". Modest though that claim might appear in relation to towering giants elsewhere, it dwarfed other buildings in Central and reset the scale for all future development. Coming in the aftermath of repercussions from China's cultural revolution, it was seen as a welcome commitment to Hong Kong's future.

Aside from sheer altitude, the building raised eyebrows for the audacity of its appearance. Spurning conventional forms, Jim Kinoshita of Palmer and Turner opted for circular windows inset into a tiled concrete façade, influenced by the cross-section of China's most ancient and versatile building material, the revered bamboo. And indeed round "moon gates" had long held an honoured place in ancient Chinese architectural tradition, being discreetly used, for hundreds of years, to offer pleasing prospects of landscaped gardens free from the rigid constraints of box-frame portals. But they had never before been employed in a tower block to frame the very different panorama of a modern city.

Hong Kong Land had no difficulty finding tenants for its flagship building, whose unrestricted views of the harbour, enclosed in large, spherical vignettes, served as a backdrop to many a personality profile on the covers of leading business magazines. So many of Jardine House's prestigious occupants were connected with the city's quickening financial tempo that the building itself was seen as playing a key role in Hong Kong's movement from a purely industrial economy to increasing status in the mercantile world. Suddenly the windows took on a new symbolism. They were seen as giant coins.

The cladding acquired a less auspicious reputation when tiles began to fall away. The problem was overcome when a second skin of aluminium covered Jardine House, more effectively complementing its garden surrounds, featuring (below) the giant "Double Oval" sculpture by Henry Moore.

EXCHANGE SQUARE

8 Connaught Place, Central

Heads rolled when Hongkong Land Limited discovered that at four and three quarter billion Hong Kong dollars, it had paid well over the prevailing market rate for a promenade site fronting Connaught Road and its pedestrian walkway. To recuperate some of that outlay as rapidly as possible, it pressed ahead with the first phase of its Exchange Square development, intent on achieving twin state-of-the-art towers that would serve as the flagship for the biggest property developer in Central.

The political climate was not conducive to rapid occupation of the most forward looking office accommodation of its time. Britain's Prime Minister, Margaret Thatcher, had just returned from an ill-starred visit to Beijing where she was unsuccessful in her attempt to persuade Chinese Premier Deng Xiaoping to renew the New Territories lease. The building was nearing completion, with the newly unified Stock Exchange and the American Club as sole confirmed occupants, when management embarked on a no-holds-barred marketing drive that included Hong Kong's first "virtual reality" presentation, subjecting visitors to a foretaste of the finished development.

The fact that Exchange Square can still command the city's most expensive office rentals is less a testament to showmanship than to a superb location combined with architectural forms best suited to its possibilities. Poised at walkway level, on a podium over Central's massive bus terminus, it offered architect Remo Riva the opportunity to develop a self-contained urban environment which, when the smaller third tower was completed, stood in its own landscaped gardens featuring impressive sculptures by such renowned artists as Henry Moore, Ju Ming and Dame Elisabeth Frink.

Talking lifts whisk tenants at high speed through fifty-two floors in a beautifully articulated geometry of circles, rectilinear and curvilinear forms, all faced in alternating layers of pink granite and silver reflective glass that mirror cloudscapes and sunsets and bask in the glow of spotlights.

INTERNATIONAL FINANCE CENTRE

1 Harbour View Street, Central

Hong Kong's sheer volume of people, taken at the flood, forms rivers that carve their own courses, forever seeking the least obstructed flow. From Mid-Levels to waterfront ferry piers and public transportation systems, this ceaseless flux has hewn channels like stream beds through descending tiers of the city, wearing smooth its stairways and inclined cross-streets through generations of shuffling feet.

Conscious of this movement, Rocco Yim, collaborating with Cesar Pelli on the International Finance Centre component of his design for the Airport Railway Station and its associated development, decided to aid rather than impede its passage. His objective was to integrate the tower concourse with the prevailing pedestrian network in a seamless transition from high-rise to rail terminus, shopping arcades and pedestrian bridges. Upper levels of the tower, sheathed in pearl coloured aluminium mullions, taper inwards with the classical contours one associates more with Chicago or New York.

Integration, Yim believes, is the key to Hong Kong's urban identity. He once delivered a paper on the aesthetics of fluidity, postulating that a mass movement of people, on the scale one finds in a typical Hong Kong lunch hour, develops its own dynamic, ignored to one's cost.

Hong Kong born and educated, Yim developed an early interest in art, but quickly realizing it was unlikely to offer a lucrative career, turned instead to architecture, finding in that discipline an alliance of art and science that furnished art with a practical application, demanding a balance between rational and creative thought. Graduating from the University of Hong Kong School of Architecture, he joined Spence Robinson in 1976 and won his first independent commission in 1979, producing a design for a Kowloon commercial centre that earned him a certificate of merit from the Hong Kong Institute of Architects. Since then the sky has been his limit.

THE CENTRE
99 Queen's Road Central

Flanked by Queen's and Des Voeux Roads Central, Jubilee Street and Gilman's Bazaar, a warren of alleyways and dilapidated buildings lay sorely in need of urban renewal by the Land Development Corporation. But the process of acquiring one of the oldest surviving quarters of Hong Kong Island proved slower than anticipated, spanning nine years and producing an irregularly shaped area of demolition, hemmed in by miscellaneous buildings of later vintage.

The ungainly result limited the options for redevelopment available to Dennis Lau and his architectural team who, after many discarded proposals, ended up designing a seventy-three-storey high-rise mounted on towering, braced girders which are clad in mirror-smooth steel and allow unobstructed pedestrian flow at ground level. Pools and shrubbery surround and blend into the lower levels, above which soars a steel and glass tower configured on a floor plan composed of two overlapping squares, one offset at an angle of forty-five degrees. No expense was spared to make this star-shaped structure – the third tallest in Hong Kong – a high-tech marvel, with emphasis on fluid illumination.

Built into the curtain wall, so they are undetectable by daylight and unobtrusive to tenants at night, a series of horizontal light bars, more closely spaced at the top than at the bottom, send pulses of ever-changing colour racing up all four "spines" emerging from the tower's underlying rectilinear form. The result is an almost hypnotic pyrotechnical display, cycling through a rainbow spectrum every six seconds. Controlled by a complex computer system, this display allows for one hundred and seventy-five different programmes, some of which are briefly demonstrated on the hour in the evening at nine, ten and eleven o'clock, when colour transitions become even more rapid and mesmerizing. So sophisticated is the circuitry for this equipment that when installed to mark the building's completion in 1998, one malfunctioning chip unleashed the chaotic effect of a supercharged karaoke juke-box experiencing a seizure, with unsettling effects for those subjected to its frenzied fluorescence.

HANG SENG BANK

83 Des Voeux Road Central

On 3 March 1933, firecrackers heralded the opening of a money-changing shop at 70 Wing Lok Street, Hong Kong. Occupying eight hundred square feet of tenement, the Hang Seng Ngan Ho, or "Evergrowing Native Bank", conducted its business on abacus boards, kept its accounts on scrolls instead of ledgers and provided its staff with meals to supplement their earnings. From such modest beginnings sprang a financial prodigy that has truly lived up to its name. Firmly enshrined in world affairs, with its index quoted alongside the Dow and Financial Times, the Hang Seng Bank possesses more than one hundred and twenty branches, and a new landmark, inaugurated in 1991, that unmistakably testifies to its importance within the community.

When the former Central Fire Station, which lay directly alongside the bank's existing but increasingly inadequate headquarters, came on the market in 1987, Hang Seng let it be known it intended to acquire the site. Bidding was fierce, with one unnamed bidder entering the fray at six hundred and eighty million Hong Kong dollars and lasting the course until Hang Seng secured the deal at eight hundred and forty million Hong Kong dollars, far more than anyone had anticipated. As evidence of its determination, the bank had already commissioned the architectural firm of Wong & Ouyang to draw up the plans.

Blueprints took account of the fact that the bank's Chairman, Sir Q.W. Lee, was much impressed by Sir Norman Foster's design for the Hang Seng's close associates in the HongkongBank. He wanted a structure that echoed the latter's suspended, column-free floors, but he would like the overall effect to be smooth and rounded with "no sharp corners". To give Sir Q.W. what he desired, architects Jackson Wong and Lam Wo Hei conceived two shining silver core shafts, vertically sandwiching a ribbed curtain wall of glass to enclose an elegant banking hall overlooked by a forty-two-foot stainless steel mural, reproducing a twelfth-century scroll by Chang Tse-tuan.

SHUN TAK CENTRE

200 Connaught Road, Central

Dissatisfied with the government's "temporary" berthing facilities for ferries to Macau, which had endured for twenty-five years in an inconvenient and overcrowded welter of piers, immigration clearance desks and waiting areas, billionaire Stanley Ho's Shun Tak Holdings Ltd decided to put the romance back into travel. They envisaged, in its place, an integrated development that would incorporate a streamlined modern terminal with twin towers containing offices and a hotel.

Spence Robinson Ltd was commissioned in 1974 to design this project, which saw completion in 1986. Since then the combined Shun Tak Centre and Macau Ferry Terminal has served Hong Kong as the maritime equivalent of its international airport. Air-conditioned bridges extend to an arrival and departure hall built out over the water and ringed with embarkation ramps for ferries, hydrofoils and turbocats, where vessels arrive and depart with the frequency of airliners.

Sheathed in mirrored curtain walling over an all-steel frame, which exposes its massive rigidity in three red layers at rooftop, midpoint and lower levels, the twin towers present an appearance of great strength and stability. Although at first sight appearing identical in their proportions and orientation, at opposite ends of a four-storey podium containing shops, restaurants, parking facilities and a transport interchange, they are in fact aligned so that the eastern presents its narrower, and the western its broader, face to the harbour. Where the former originally housed a five hundred and fifty-room hotel, both are now given over largely to office accommodation.

Connected to the heart of the city along a network of pedestrian walkways that diverge into the first floors of neighbouring buildings, the Shun Tak Centre has conspicuously achieved its developer's intentions, investing the experience of a journey to Macau – be it only over a distance of sixty kilometres – with something of the glamour and occasion that once accompanied departures in the golden age of sea travel.

THE ORIGINAL SKYWALKERS

Skywalking scaffolders still storm the heavens on trellises of bamboo that have cocooned virtually every construction since an embryonic trading outpost gained its foothold on Hong Kong's waterfront. No modern assemblies of bolted steel tubing or any other material have entirely weaned them away from time-honoured bamboo, whose sturdier segments are so durable they can survive repeated use until deemed unfit for further employment.

Treading on thin-soled slippers and interlocking their feet for better purchase on the poles, scaffolders work in well orchestrated teams, lashing together conjunctions of bamboo with bindings as they rapidly ascend to vertiginous heights. Their segmentation, into a patchwork of matching thigh-high squares, of some fresh gap in the skyline is often the first indication that something new is about to make its appearance; an invitation to "watch this space". And when construction within the scaffolding's embrace is nearing completion, the dismantling of the bamboo casing offers dramatic revelation of what has lain hidden within.

Yet too often the appearance of scaffolding around some familiar edifice portends the opposite process, serving notice that yet another landmark is about to disappear and make way for some bigger successor that will nevertheless leave an ache in the collective memory for what it has replaced.

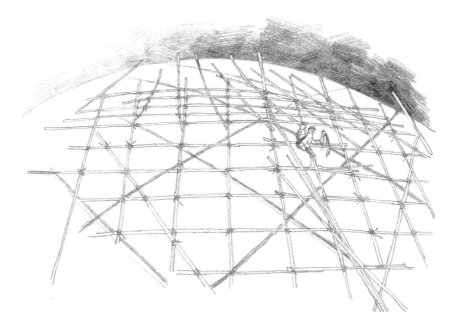

HMS TAMAR

Edinburgh Place, Central

One of the last hurdles impeding talks between the two
governments, leading up to Britain's return of Hong Kong to
Chinese sovereignty at midnight on 30 June 1997, was the vexed
question of what to do about H.M.S. Tamar. This former Joint
Defence Headquarters was named after a three-masted barque
moored offshore from 1897 to 1941, when it was scuttled to
prevent its use by invading Japanese. The vessel's role had been
to serve as "receiving ship" for the Commodore of the Fleet.

Despite having occupied the key site, in the heart of town, since
a naval dockyard was established here in 1842 – the year
Hong Kong formally became a British colony – the British were
anxious to ensure that any future military presence would be as
invisible as possible. They would have preferred to see all units
of the People's Liberation Army located well away from key
urban areas, on sites such as Stonecutters Island. But the Chinese
were adamant that they inherit the headquarters of the British
garrison – in the building named after the Prince of Wales when
he declared it open in 1979 – together with all its precincts within
the walled confines of the naval dockyard.

Having achieved their objective, the P.L.A. set out, within a year
of occupying the structure, to remove the label identifying it as
the Prince of Wales Building, but the deeply incised lettering
proved remarkably impervious, and was still recognizable as the
second anniversary of the handover approached. The fate of the
building itself hung in the balance. Designed by the Property
Services Agency of the British government, it is distinguished
only by its curiously waisted lower levels, which taper inward to
ensure against explosive damage from possible terrorist attacks.
Envying those enjoying its air-conditioned comforts, Gurkha
officers serving on the border during the final years of British rule
looked upon it with jaundiced eyes as the "inverted gin bottle".

THE PRINCE OF WALES BUILDING

HONG KONG CONVENTION AND EXHIBITION CENTRE

1 Harbour Road, Wanchai

Aerofoils poised for flight remained the one constant, from first blueprint to final reality, marking the metamorphosis of the Convention and Exhibition Centre extension. Hong Kong architects Wong & Ouyang, working with American partners Skidmore Owings & Merrill International, envisaged a roof of overlapping aerodynamic fins. Models, displayed like jewelled scarabs in the office of chief conceptualist Lam Wo Hei, all share this defining feature, variously compared to lotus petals, banana leaves and gull wings.

The team had made a successful combined bid in the aftermath of a near miss, when they were on a short list of three for the new international airport. Trade Development Council Chairman Victor Fung urged them to elevate the council's showcase into a signature building of which Hong Kong could be proud; on a par with Sydney's Opera House and the Parliament buildings in London. They faced two considerable obstacles. Firstly in regard to the site, which did not even exist when they were commissioned, and secondly in regard to time, because of a midnight deadline, on 30 June 1997, which allowed no flexibility. The extension, sited at the harbour's heart and backed by the city's most spectacular assembly of architectural features, was chosen as the setting for Hong Kong's ceremonial return to Chinese sovereignty.

To avoid any further obstruction of an already impeded harbour flow, the structure was sited on a reclaimed island, connected to the existing Trade Development Council complex by a walkway serving as an atrium bridging old and new. Upon this relatively small plot, shaped like an arrow head, are stacked three large exhibition halls, the grandest of which commands a one hundred and eighty-degree panorama of the harbour. All Hong Kong watched, spellbound, the race against time, through weeks of monsoon rains, from the start of planning in April 1994, when no site existed, to the solemn moment when the historic handover ended one hundred and fifty years of British rule.

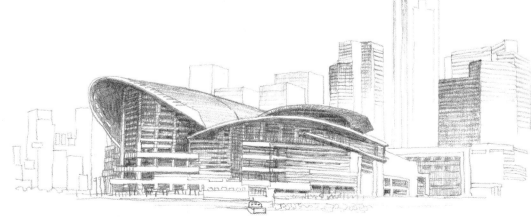

CENTRAL PLAZA

18 Harbour Road, Wanchai

The competitive urge to stand taller than the rest, which long declined elsewhere in the world but still holds Asia in thrall, has not spared Hong Kong. The new Bank of China tower upped the stakes in the late eighties, but was quickly overtaken by Central Plaza, inaugurated in 1992. The latter briefly claimed to be the tallest structure outside North America before a pair of giant binoculars in Kuala Lumpur usurped its place. However, Central Plaza remains the second tallest reinforced concrete building in the world, deferring to only one other in that material, located in Guangzhou, South China, designed by Dennis Lau.

Originally the developers of Central Plaza, Sun Hung Kai and Sino Land, wanted a ninety-two-storey tower in conventional steel and glass, but the bottom dropped out of the market following the 1989 incident at Tiananmen Square, compelling the partnership of developers to opt instead for seventy-eight storeys in reinforced concrete at an overall saving of some two hundred and fifty million Hong Kong dollars. Lau confronted the problem of how to secure the best harbour views, so dear to the heart of any Hong Kong realtor. The site he worked with was previously a public park, buried behind ramparts of the original Convention and Exhibition Centre for which he had earlier been responsible.

He settled for a triangular floor plan, offering optimal "view corridors" between adjacent buildings, and he eliminated the three points this geometry produced to make it more friendly to any neighbours concerned with the inauspicious feng shui implications of "dagger blades". By blunting each apex, and incorporating a triangular service core, he achieved a floor plan that could be conveniently configured in three interlocking rectangles for greater economy of space. And, instead of abruptly terminating the building at its crest, he drew the three corners into a stepped pyramid, housing a superb entertainment penthouse for its developers and crowned by a slender spire that ripples with light to clock the hours.

FAR EAST FINANCE CENTRE

16 Harcourt Road, Central

Planned in the seventies, when Hong Kong was far less driven
to architectural experimentation than it is today, the Far East
Finance Centre betrays its modest aims and clear-cut objectives.
Its developers wanted a straightforward high-rise on a relatively
small site, with a total space of no more than ten thousand square
feet per floor, which they could dispose of relatively quickly
through strata-titled sales. They also wanted it in gold,
universally recognized – but probably more so by the Chinese
than any other people – as the symbol of wealth.

Designed by Wong & Ouyang, who were later commissioned
to produce blueprints for almost all of its immediate
neighbours, the fifty-storey tower was completed in a year, and
"priced to sell", rapidly achieving its goal by finding ready
buyers in an expanding market for such office accommodation.
Built on caisson pilings, which have long since been banned
in Hong Kong because of the risk of soil subsidence trapping
workers in their cylindrical shafts, it was, in its time, one of the
few steel-frame buildings to make a mark on the local skyline.

The startling gold-tinted glass cladding instantly earned the
structure its popular nickname, "The Amah's Tooth". In its
defence, architect Lam Wo Hei points out that, aside from
making an arresting contribution to the assembly of buildings
fronting the Hong Kong Island promenade, the building's façade
– still largely unobstructed in its command of fine harbour
prospects – serves to shield occupants from direct sunlight
and thereby enhances energy efficiency. The structure is so
fortuitously sited that from May to October it glows in the rising
sun and emblazons its gilded seal upon the harbour.

CITIC TOWER

1 Tim Mei Avenue, Central

The developers of CITIC Tower held an international competition to determine who should design it. The winner, Hong Kong's veteran architectural firm of Palmer and Turner, was faced with a difficult triangular site and restraints on the building's height. It met these limitations with a design that spiralled from a triangular base to a V-shape, eventually tapering to a lozenge along just one side of the site's curious alignment.

The tower's rounded corners are vertically articulated, to contrast with the horizontal definition of the flat faces between; a feature which achieves its best impact when subjected to the spotlights that nightly illuminate all façades. Because hanging gardens intersperse these façades at different elevations, no two views of the building are alike, no matter what the vantage point. The result is a structure of interest and variety, like an interlocking Chinese puzzle whose elements one is compelled to reconfigure when the perspective shifts.

Its developers, CITIC Pacific, trading arm of the State Council of China, were anxious to complete the project in time to mark Hong Kong's return to Chinese sovereignty at midnight on 30 June 1997. Although it failed to fully achieve this objective, CITIC Tower's upper levels provided a perfect vantage point from which to view the sunset parade, in pouring rain, which immediately preceded that landmark event as a farewell to one hundred and fifty years of British rule. It also served as an observation platform when the Royal yacht *Britannia* sailed out of the harbour on its last voyage, bearing with it the Queen's emissary and Hong Kong's last governor.

LIPPO CENTRE

89 Queensway, Central

When the Mass Transit Railway completed excavation of its link between Central and Admiralty stations it covered its tracks with a concrete base and foundations for two towers straddling the line. This precondition, together with a requirement to accommodate a key telephone exchange, governed the sale of the site by auction in 1985.

Heading the consortium that purchased it, Indonesian developer Henry Kwee was persuaded by his American-educated sons to engage as design adviser renowned American architect Paul Rudolph, dean of Yale's school of architecture. Rudolph, then in his seventies, worked harmoniously with Hong Kong architects Wong & Ouyang, who adapted well to his input. The idea of producing vertical glass boxes, in the prevailing local style of the period, was anathema to the American. His sculptural approach to architecture influenced the interlocking cubic shapes of the twin glass-clad towers which, when Australian entrepreneur Alan Bond bought the development shortly before completion, became known as the cuddling koala bears.

Poised on giant thirty-metre columns above a sweep of stairs ascending from Queensway, the building did not long carry its name as the Bond Centre. Although the Lippo organization acquired naming rights, the bulk of the floor space is divided between a number of owners; a situation which has led to a lack of co-ordinated maintenance.

One of the original architects Lam Wo Hei delights in explaining the mystery of what happened to the obligatory telephone exchange. Studied closely, the building's imposing atrium is seen to be roofed in a thick podium slab. Inside this is buried the largely electronic facility. And the inspiration for the cubist forms that give the towers their distinctive shape? It derives, he assures us, more from music than from anything graphically representational, reflecting the rhythm and pace of the city it serves to embellish.

PACIFIC PLACE

88 Queensway, Central

Observers who see Pacific Place as the largest, most versatile and best integrated urban enclave in the city centre would be surprised to learn it is the consequence of two separate land purchases by Swire Properties in 1985 and 1986, when the government auctioned, piecemeal, two adjoining sites at the foot of a former military barracks. Planning for the first phase was already well advanced when it became necessary to incorporate the second, and larger acquisition. The former, comprising the JW Marriott Hotel and an office tower known as One Pacific Place, was aligned along Queensway whereas phase two, accommodating the Conrad International and Island Shangri-La hotels, embraced a large chunk of steeply inclined terrain southwest of that site.

Pondering how to make a cohesive whole of these two elements, architects Jackson Wong and Lam Wo Hei of Wong & Ouyang, focused on providing access routes to the adjoining Admiralty MTR station and its ancillary bus terminal; one at the western end crossing the Queensway thoroughfare on a broad, and heavily used pedestrian footbridge, and the other at the eastern end tunneling under the road. Arching in a horseshoe from these pivotal points, a three-level shopping arcade, crisscrossed with escalators intersecting a central airwell, entices shoppers into its brightly lit parabola, affording lift access to all three hotels rising from the podium's landscaped surface.

To achieve this it was necessary to dig out the hillside, exposing ancient underground bunkers, one of which housed a prewar emergency headquarters for the combined services, later occupied by Japanese forces in World War II. As a safeguard, Taoist monks exorcised this military past. More problematic was the government's insistence that an ancient banyan should remain at the heart of the excavation. To overcome this hurdle, Swire Properties built the world's most expensive plant pot, supporting the tree in a concrete container while they burrowed underneath for the three-level shopping arcade and two-level, five hundred-bay car park. This costly testament to environmental preservation survives as a gem in the clasp composed of its orbital towers.

ACADEMY FOR PERFORMING ARTS

1 Gloucester Road, Wanchai

Winning a contest for the design of a proposed Academy for Performing Arts, Simon Kwan & Associates Ltd were faced with the daunting problem of where to place its foundations. The site straddled major underground services, including water and sewage mains, and the Mass Transit Rail route to Tsim Sha Tsui. To keep the structure's pilings well clear of these, he opted for a design bisected at an angle, across two opposing corners of a square, by an access road. The two triangles resulting from this configuration are united across the roadway in a building which, despite an external appearance dominated by triangular forms, is composed almost entirely of conventional rectangular spaces.

The one exception that replicates the external theme is the structure's beautifully conceived core, a triangular atrium in which Simon Kwan amasses all the space allocated for separate lobbies originally envisaged for the various theatres. This atrium, sunlit by glass panels in a roof of terraced planes, is the building's most striking feature, a public area from which concert and theatre goers are reluctantly summoned for the second half of their respective entertainments.

Surrounding this space are a concert hall, drama theatre, studio theatre for productions "in the round", rehearsal and recording hall, dance studio, library and reference centre, and student common room. To minimize acoustical interference, these facilities – all of which contribute to the academy's mission of teaching promising Asian youngsters the performing arts – are built on "floating" structures. Such soundproofing was vital, given the proximity of major traffic arteries, sea lanes, an underground railway and a helicopter landing pad.

Although his two basically triangular shapes surrendered the maximum usable cubic space, leaving only residual points to house stairwells and service elements, Simon Kwan was determined to exploit their design potential. When viewed from outside, the building bristles with almost razor-sharp edges that contribute an emphatic identity, complemented by similarly triangular window panes and steel framework over the outdoor theatre.

JAMIA MOSQUE

Shelly Street

Jamia Mosque Seamen from the Indian sub-continent were among the first to sail into Hong Kong harbour aboard British ships. Many served on tea clippers from Calcutta and other ports, increasing numbers of them settling in the area which derived its appellation from this influx, namely Lower Lascar Road, now popularly known as Cat Street. Those of the Muslim faith worshipped in the open street, much to the surprise of local Chinese who had never before witnessed prayer mats rolled out for this purpose.

To cater to the spiritual needs of the Islamic community, a mosque was established on its present site in 1890. Its congregation numbered immigrants from Chinese Turkistan, Burma, Ceylon, Indo-China and southern Russia, but the largest complement came from Indians recruited as police constables, marine and prison guards, watchmen, ferry supervisors and government drivers. In 1896 a much larger Moorish-style mosque was erected at the corner of Austin and Nathan roads for Muslim soldiers garrisoned in Kowloon. This prompted the Hong Kong Island Muslim community to raise funds for the replacement of hopelessly inadequate premises bordering Shelly and Mosque streets; a drive which resulted in the inauguration of the present Jamia Mosque in 1915.

Capable of accommodating a congregation of four hundred, its grounds embrace gardens, a ceremonial fountain for the spiritual cleansing of feet and hands before prayer, changing rooms for worship, and a Yatim Khana (home for widows and children). The mosque's motto is "Hold fast unto the rope of Allah".

Syed Mohammed Noor Shah was the Jamia Mosque's first imam. He arrived in Hong Kong during World War I as a military imam with the 2nd Punjab Regiment and retired in 1948, returning to Rawalpindi. He was known for his skills in Arabic calligraphy and in knotting Turkish-style prayer caps which he generously handed out as transit gifts to Muslims passing through Hong Kong on their way to China.

ST JOHN'S BUILDING

33 Garden Road, Central

As if to underline the impermanence of Hong Kong architecture, the second building to occupy the site of the lower Peak Tram station, a medium-rise block containing the Four Seasons restaurant and residential apartments, had stood barely a decade when its owners decided it wasn't sufficiently large, grand and profitable. Commissioned in 1981 to replace it with an office tower, Anthony Ng, then a founder and director of KNW Architects and Engineers Ltd, worked with a narrow site, steeply inclined and islanded by an encircling nexus of arterial and slip roads.

His proposed solution was so startling that his clients doubted its viability. He proposed wrapping the structure's slender profile in prefabricated cast aluminium cladding, whose panels would come preassembled, enclosing windows so stable and perfectly sealed they could safely curve around the building's corners. Architect Ng did his homework to ensure this fabric, reminiscent of an aircraft fuselage, would be typhoon proof. He subjected it to rain and gale in a wind tunnel and, when one of the panels failed, totally redesigned the fittings to ensure against any recurrence. In the years since the project's completion in 1983, no window breakage or leakage has occurred.

Ng derived greatest satisfaction from the challenge of building atop a tram terminus. Having lived for a year in Rome, where he fell in love with classical form, he recalled in particular his fascination with the grand stairway leading up to the church of Santa Maria Maggiore. This led him to devise a headland jutting out from the northern face of St John's, cascading in a curved flight of steps alongside a terraced waterfall from a fountain at the apex. In doing so he replaced an unsightly, angular descent with one of the building's strongest features, complemented at the upper end of the site by a banyan tree he took pains to preserve. The result has enhanced its surroundings and greatly dignified one of the island's principal commuter routes.

THE PEAK TOWER

128 Peak Road, The Peak

The hierarchy of social strata in early colonial Hong Kong was measured in contour lines. The higher one aspired, the greater the geographical elevation required of one's domicile. Despite prolonged immersion in cloud for large parts of each calendar year, the prominence above the city of Victoria was named The Peak because it defined the summit of social attainment. Its exclusivity was such that for many years Chinese were debarred from living there. Like Olympian gods deigning to descend among mere mortals, its denizens would commute by the funicular railway inaugurated in 1888 and described by Kipling as "a tramway that stood on its head and waved its feet in the mist."

But once this transportation made it both readily accessible and popular, The Peak replaced exclusivity with mass appeal, courting residents from lower levels together with tourists. Regular commuters were discommoded by having to share their tram with "day trippers" heading for cafeterias, penny-slot telescopes, picture postcards and curio stalls. To house these attractions in more orderly surroundings, the Peak Tramways Company commissioned a series of upper terminal buildings, each contributing a progressively grander and more conspicuous presence on the skyline. The latest version, commissioned in 1991 and completed in 1995, is described by its creator, Terry Farrell, as "open to many readings and interpretations; of boat, bird, bowl, open hands."

It is also reminiscent, he says, of traditional Chinese architectural precedents, of solid base, open podium and floating roof with upswept eaves which make it appear to float above ground. Some have likened it to an urn, in votive offering to the gods of commerce. For functional purposes, the structure is divided into two principal elements; the podium and the bowl. The former houses the upper tram station, accessed at different levels for embarkation and disembarkation, and associated with extensive outlets for retail enterprise. The latter contains restaurants offering spectacular views of the city below and the harbour beyond.

THE PENINSULA

Salisbury Road, Kowloon

Hong Kong was filled with a mixture of relief and trepidation when The Peninsula announced that, while it would not disappear under demolition hammers, it intended to expand. The whole city had developed an almost proprietary interest in its oldest and most distinguished hotel whose history, since it opened its doors in 1928, spanned the ages of trans-continental rail and trans-oceanic jet travel.

Commissioned to produce a design that would greatly increase floor space while retaining the flavour of the original H-block, architect Rocco Yim initially opted for twin towers, covering the forecourt and – he still believes – achieving a more intense dialogue between old and new. However, halfway through the planning stage, the government lifted restraints on building heights in Kowloon, enabling the management to opt for a higher, single tower to replace the podium at the rear and to cantilever out over part of the existing structure.

The challenge was to meld the two as seamlessly as possible, given the awkward fact that heights and spatial dimensions of the new floors would be considerably different from those of the original structure which was approved more than sixty years earlier. It was vital that the ground and first floors in particular, containing the main public and dining areas, should be freely interconnected, with the next priority being to afford similarly unrestricted access to the roof of the old block from the new indoor swimming pool.

Yim regards the latter achievement as the hotel's most dramatic space. Emerging on to the rooftop sun deck, the swimmer is engulfed in the entire panorama of harbour and island backdrop, and is immediately conscious of the felicitous amalgam of past and present. Only at close quarters does it become unmistakably apparent that, where the brickwork of the old building remains clad in Shanghai plaster, the tower is faced with factory produced aluminium panels prefabricated in Japan. The Peninsula provides a rare example of an adaptation that, far from compromising the appeal of the original, offers a greater magnet for those who might otherwise regard it only as a souvenir of faded glories.

THE REPULSE BAY

109 Repulse Bay Road

Demolition of the Repulse Bay Hotel in 1982 met with surprisingly concerted opposition from a community that had seemed inured to the loss of such links with its past. Built in 1922, the hotel had sheltered the last remnants of Allied troops defending the island against Japanese invaders. Dismay verged on anger when a general economic downturn delayed evidence of its replacement. Having been advised that the structure must go if its environs were to be redeveloped, Hong Kong and Shanghai Hotels found themselves in a dilemma.

They resolved it by engaging Anthony Ng of Kwan Ng Wong & Associates, who pointed out they could have preserved the beloved landmark. When he demonstrated how they could enshrine something of the spirit of that structure in a contemporary replacement, group chairman Michael Kadoorie wanted him to go further by restoring as much as possible of the look and style of the original. Many of the hotel's fittings, including doors and architectural embellishments, were stored in an adjoining car park. With the aid of photographs, architect Ng constructed models of the vanished colonial relic to determine what could be resurrected. The resulting renaissance gave back to Hong Kong a familiar visage fronting a wholly modern interior, in a blend of old and new.

As backdrop, Ng devised four staggered residential towers, their edges softened and screened by an undulating façade which echoed the contours of the bay and served to shade the apartments within. It was Kadoorie again who, having seen something similar in Florida, suggested a massive inset of free space, framing the sky and hills beyond through a picture window. Much earlier, famed architect Le Corbusier had proposed a similar inset for a hotel in Paris. Together with the structure's various "sky gardens", located at different levels to punctuate the flowing lines of the whole, this borrowed expression contributes to what Ng sees as the "evolving language of architecture".

PARKVIEW

88 Tai Tam Reservoir Road

Sited on the edge of the Tai Tam country park, the Parkview residential development provoked consternation among environmentalists concerned for its proximity to one of Hong Kong Island's sacred and tenaciously defended "green lungs". Architects Wong Tung & Partners were tasked to ensure that, while maintaining empathy with its setting, Parkview would be demonstrably emphatic in its design. The latter objective was strikingly achieved by installing eighteen towers grouped in seven clusters, rising from a landscaped podium and pushed to the boundaries of the five and a half hectare plot. In the words of a Wong Tung group Deputy Director, the intention of building along the perimeter of the site was to create "the largest uninterrupted area of landscaping that could be tied in with that of the surrounding country park".

Within this enclosure, atop three levels of car park, lie tennis courts, swimming pools, a children's playground, club house and terraced gardens with fountains and waterfalls, one of which screens the windows of an indoor health club. Other facilities include squash courts, a racquetball court, gymnasium, aerobics and table tennis rooms. Elsewhere under the podium is a supermarket large enough to serve Parkview's four thousand residents and the surrounding neighbourhood. In many respects, the complex epitomizes Hong Kong's unique approach to stacked development as a solution to high density housing.

Restaurants and a boardroom span the gateway frontage of the complex, offering dramatic views across the adjacent country park towards Happy Valley and the harbour beyond. So elevated is the site on Hong Kong Island's mountainous spine, and so sheer are the ramparts of its encircling tower blocks, that the project, visible for miles, commands the skyline like some towering Mediaeval fortress.

ECHOES
OF EDWARDIAN
ELEGANCE

35 Bonham Road, Pokfulam

Stringent building regulations were introduced in 1903,
governing the height and general dimensions of Hong Kong's
residential buildings. The objective was to avoid repetitions of
disastrous outbreaks of bubonic plague and other infectious
diseases arising from the congested and unsanitary development
that had occurred in the previous century. New buildings would
be no higher than four storeys, or 23.2 metres in total. Depths of
more than 12.2 metres were permissible only if every floor was
generously provided with windows to ensure adequate lighting.

Within these constraints, domestic buildings of elegant
proportions, with deep, colonnaded and arched balconies, began
to replace the previous clutter that had endeavoured to cope with
huge influxes of immigrants arriving from the mainland. Strong
bonds of sentimental attachment were formed between these new
domiciles and the families fortunate enough to occupy them;
bonds that in many cases have lasted through generations to
ensure the survival of especially beloved tenement homes such as
35 Bonham Road.

While balconies alternately serve as play pens for children,
drying areas for laundry lines and observation points from
which to survey life passing by beneath, they also afford space
for hanging gardens of pot plants to screen occupants from
increasingly intrusive and overbearing structures crowding into
the neighbourhood. Barriers of palm and fern help preserve the
illusion that all is as it was; that skylines have not been elevated
to impossible heights and the heavens remain unstormed by cliffs
of steel and glass.

UNIVERSITY OF HONG KONG

Pokfulum Road, Hong Kong

Even missionaries voiced misgivings when Governor Sir Frederick Lugard (1908-1912) proposed that Hong Kong should have its own university. They feared it would foster a movement of rebellion and anarchy. Local Chinese were hardly less suspicious, being reluctant to concede the advantages of an English education when they regarded their own as infinitely superior.

Among those with whom the concept found favour was Dr Sun Yat-sen, at that time fulfilling the missionaries' worst fears by using Hong Kong as a base from which to instigate the overthrow of China's Manchu government.

Hong Kong had played a crucial role in Dr Sun's political development. At the age of seventeen, he had been sent to school here to place him beyond the reach of irate officials in Xiangshan County, Guangdong Province, where he damaged idols in the local temple. After two years of high school education, followed by a six-month spell in Honolulu, he entered the Hong Kong College of Medicine for Chinese and graduated in July 1892.

The school from which he launched his college career was later renamed Victoria College and finally Queen's College which, together with the College for Medicine, then constituted the only avenues open to Chinese for an English education.

The government having provided the site at Pok Fu Lam, Governor Lugard aimed to finance the university through private subscription, but Hong Kong was going through a recession at the time and the response proved lukewarm until Chinese businessman Ng Li-hang contributed fifty thousand Hong Kong dollars. A personal appeal by Lady Lugard led a wealthy Parsee, HN Mody, to donate one hundred fifty thousand Hong Kong dollars for construction, together with a thirty thousand Hong Kong dollars endowment. Other donations followed, enabling the university to open in 1913.

The main hall and library were wrecked during the Japanese occupation, and much of the regalia looted. But it reopened its doors in 1948 and today the University of Hong Kong enrols over fourteen thousand students in nine faculties.

DOUGLAS CASTLE

University Grounds, Pokfulum

From palatial residence to printing press to student dormitory,
Douglas Castle has outlived many occupants, undergone at least
three metamorphoses and witnessed numerous changes of name
and surroundings. Yet its crenellated towers, gothic arches and
extravagant architecture have survived, virtually unchanged, since
it began life in 1861 as residence and headquarters of John
Douglas Lapraik. Within sixteen years of arriving in Hong Kong in
1843, Lapraik graduated from watchmaker's assistant to his own
watchmaking business. In gratitude to the city that encouraged
his meteoric rise, he donated a clock tower in 1862 which stood,
elegantly Victorian, on a traffic island at the corner of Queen's and
Pedder streets until demolished because it was a traffic hazard.
By1870 he had become owner of eight coastal steamers, forming
the nucleus of the Douglas Steamship Company.

In 1894 his castle was sold to the Societe des Missions Etrangeres
de Paris, who renamed it Nazareth House and enlarged it to
incorporate a gothic chapel and crypt. In the main body of the
building they established a printing workshop producing sixty
thousand religious tracts and related publications each year in
as many as twenty-eight languages. Their energetic publishing
enterprise was interrupted only by World War II, when Japanese
occupation forces allowed the French fathers to remain in
residence, but denied them permission to proselytize.

In 1954 Nazareth House was purchased by the University of Hong
Kong as a hall of residence for male students. The chapel, with
vaulted ceiling, stained glass windows and heavy wooden beams,
became a dining hall and the crypt was converted into a common
room. Under the name of University Hall, the exuberantly
anachronistic building continues to reward incumbents for their
submission to chilly rooms and draughty corridors by offering
them a position of secluded yet commanding prominence, amid a
grove of trees fronted by gardens that overlook splendid views of
the harbour's western approaches.

HONG KONG MUSEUM OF MEDICAL SCIENCES

2 Caine Lane, Mid-Levels

In 1894, two scientists – a Japanese and a Swiss – independently toiled to discover the cause of a ferocious outbreak of bubonic plague in the Tai Ping Shan quarter of Hong Kong Island. Volunteers of the Shropshire Light Infantry were provoking intense hostility with remedial disinfectant measures and their search for victims. Unwilling to surrender their dead for summary disposal in ditches covered with quicklime, residents of the overcrowded community were smuggling both the stricken and the corpses from house to house to spare them denial of a dignified burial according to Chinese custom.

Afforded the cooperation of local medical authorities, Shibasaburo Kitasato was the first to announce he had isolated the causative organism, though he was uncertain what type of bacteria he had discovered. Within days Alexandre Yersin, refusing the help his rival received, provided the first accurate description and culture of the plague bacillus that now bears his name, *Yersinia pestis*.

The achievements of both is commemorated in the former Pathological Institute, founded in 1905 and restored in 1996 as the home of Hong Kong's Museum of Medical Sciences. The building's modest entrance belies the crucial laboratory work carried out over the many years when the institute produced vaccines to counter various infectious diseases, including smallpox. Above this unimposing doorway is an elaborate triptych of window crowned by a fan pediment incorporating a circular skylight. The flanking east and west façades are set with arched verandahs. Supported on brick buttresses, the elegant cast-iron balconies of the north façade overlook the totally redeveloped Tai Ping Shan area, once ravaged by onslaughts of the scourge that led to the building's inception.

TING KAU BRIDGE
The Rambler Channel

Chief Highways Engineer Wai Chi Sing and his team, examining tenders for design and construction of a new bridge from Tsing Yi Island to Ting Kau, as part of the projected Route 3 to Yuen Long, took a tremendous guarded leap of faith when they chose, from seven submissions by international consortia, a concept that had never been tested elsewhere. Whereas four of the submissions were for conventional suspension or cable stayed bridges, requiring extended approach viaducts that would effectively block off half of Rambler Channel, the other three proposed spanning the channel's full width with three cable stayed tower links. Two of the latter opted for standard portal towers, and only one envisaged single towers, whose cables would grip both sides of the flanking bridge decks.

The question was whether the central tower, lacking the shore-based anchorage points of the other two, would prove strong enough to sustain the tremendous loads entailed. German designer Schlaich Bergermann, employed by Ting Kau Contractors Joint Venture, envisaged both transverse and longitudinal cables. The transverse system resembles a sailboat rig, running from the central tower mast to the outer ends of a cross strut under the road decks and then in again to grip the tower footings. Anchored to the other two towers, the longitudinal stay cables are each four hundred and sixty-five metres, the longest ever installed on a bridge.

Scepticism was voiced as to the outcome, but when the bridge was inaugurated on 5 May 1998, it elicited nothing but praise. Engineers worldwide came to marvel at its grace and symmetry, far exceeding the more conventional designs of its two neighbours, the giant Tsing Ma suspension bridge and its ancillary, the Kap Shui Mun bridge at the other end of the Lantau Fixed Crossing. All three bridges, serving as conduits for an intricate nexus of highways, collectively straddle the sea, road and air routes to China, constituting a massive gateway to the world's emerging superpower.

THE GREAT BUDDHA
Lantau Island

The skills of architect Peter Ng Pin-kin, and of craftsmen who worked on China's space rockets, went into the construction of the world's largest outdoor bronze Buddha, the first that anyone, anywhere, had attempted in more than a thousand years.

Ng was called in when monks of Po Lin Monastery, on Lantau Island, having spent seven years selecting a suitable site on nearby Muk Yu Hill, discarded an earlier design in favour of one too heavy for its foundations. Instead of reinforced concrete, he persuaded them to opt for a structural steel frame supporting cast bronze, moulded in sections like the Great Buddha of Kamakura.

The contract that transformed his concept into reality went to the China Aeronautics Science and Technology Consultant Corporation who took three months, working from a one-in-five scale model, to perfect the full-size design. The Chenguang Machinery Manufacturing Company in Nanjing constructed individual moulds for the two hundred and two bronze sections, each about a centimetre thick and weighing eight hundred kilograms. Inevitably the crucial focus was Buddha's face, cast in one piece measuring 5.8 by 4.8 metres.

This visage proved too heavy for any helicopter to convey to the site. The only alternative meant closing off, for three nights, all roads leading to the monastery to allow for dismantling of lamp posts, telephone and electricity services that might impede the over-sized vehicles transporting this exceptional cargo. Even when the statue was finally assembled on its imposing mountain fastness, its inauguration was delayed for three years to permit expansion of the access route from a circuitous track to a dual carriageway.

Finally, on 29 December 1993, an assembly of ten thousand watched monks from thirteen countries lead prayers of dedication. Towering above them, the Tian Tin Buddha, betraying no evidence of the technological expertise that brought it into existence, looked serenely undisturbed, as if meditating through centuries of mist-wrapped seclusion among the folded green raiments of mountainous Lantau.

HONG KONG INTERNATIONAL AIRPORT

8 Chun Yue Road, Lantau

Viewed from above, the billowing wingspread contours of the terminal building of Hong Kong International Airport acquire the delicacy of a fragile aeronautical device that launched pioneer aviators into history books, and the world into a love affair with the age of flight.

Untrammelled space, height and luminosity were the objectives of architect Norman Foster, who achieved his purpose with immense curvatures of glassed roof, shielded from heat and glare yet admitting enough of the sky beyond to encourage a sense that outward bound passengers already have one foot in the clouds. Echoing this uplift of spirits and expectations, Australian artist Michael Santry's suspended sailcloth panels arch across the main concourse leading to the departure gates.

Reaching for the stars, with the most costly and ambitious investment the world had ever seen, the whole enterprise looked at one stage as if it would be interminably mired in politics and controversy. First envisaged in the late seventies as a replacement for the convenient but hair-raising Kai Tak runway, shoehorned into the crook of Kowloon Bay, the new airport called for demolition of the former island of Chek Lap Kok in the Lantau Channel. Though a severe recession prompted former Financial Secretary Sir John Bremridge to scrap the project in 1984, it was resurrected again, and publicly announced in 1989 as a confidence booster, in the aftermath of Tienanmen Square.

Protracted negotiations ensued with China over the need for so costly an undertaking, and contention was hotly revived when the project was seen to be rushed to completion in time for China's President Jiang Zemin to depart on 2 July 1998, after his visit to commemorate the first anniversary of the Special Administrative Region. The new airport has since attracted more praise than brickbats. A recent international conference of engineers in Las Vegas voted it seventh on a list of the top ten construction achievements of the twentieth century.

PO LIN MONASTERY
Lantau Island

Seekers after spiritual seclusion have long carved sandal-shod footpaths into the green robed hills of Lantau Island, whose folds shroud more than a hundred Buddhist monasteries of varying size and antiquity. Here, until the new international airport brought its complex infrastructure of air, road and rail links to assail Lantau's hitherto pristine insularity, it was possible to withdraw among clouded peaks, severing all ties with that urgent metropolis just a ferry ride away.

The largest and most frequented of these retreats is the Precious Lotus, or Po Lin Monastery, founded by three monks who settled here in 1905. The location, a remote plateau under the brow of Lantau *(Broken Head)* Peak, was ideally suited for their reclusive meditations, but they could not preclude others of similar mind from joining them. At first this eyrie could only be attained by a tortuous pilgrim's path from the fishing village of Tai O, but a winding dual-lane highway now brings tourists by the coach load.

Officially declared a monastery in 1927, Po Lin remained a group of modest buildings until the late 1960s, when two million Hong Kong dollars was raised in donations for a two-storey temple, a sub-temple and two pavilions. Inaugurated in 1970, the enlarged complex is distinctive for its tiled roofs, their endings upturned over vermilion walls and pillars, set on granite platforms ascended by stone-balustraded stairs. The main temple houses three Buddhas seated on lotus flowers, each ten feet high. Centre stage is Sakyamuni, founder of Buddhism. On the right is Amitabha, Lord of the Western Paradise, and on the left the Healing Buddha.

Every three years, novice monks gather here for the Hoi Gai initiation ceremony, many travelling from far-flung corners of the world. Two months of prayer, fasting and recitation of the sutras culminate in a ceremony at which they submit their shaven heads to burning joss sticks to brand them as full-fledged monks.

TUNG CHUNG FORT

Lantau Island

Alarmed by reports of rampant piracy in the Pearl River estuary and Lantau Channel, Viceroy Jiang You Tien proposed, in 1817, the construction of eight guardhouses, two batteries and an ammunition store at Tung Chung, on Lantau Island. According to historical records, at least three forts were built in close proximity, manned by thirty soldiers under one officer to form a strategic part of the island's defences.

The sole surviving structure, fitted with eighteen cannons – of which only six are on display today – remained a stronghold until 1898, when Lantau became absorbed into the territories leased to Britain and the Royal Navy took over anti-piracy duties. Tung Chung fort then became a police station, manned by Indian constables, and in 1938 was converted into a summer school for local children, with six classrooms built in the inner courtyard. During World War II it quartered troops of the Japanese occupation forces.

Still in remarkable condition, the structure occupies a site of seventy by eighty metres, enclosed by substantial walls of well-dressed granite, with arches to east and west and the main arch facing north, towards the island of Chek Lap Kok now levelled to serve as Hong Kong's international airport. In 1983 the fort was declared a protected monument.

FAN LAU FORT

Lantau Island

Seventy metres above sea level at the southwest tip of Lantau Island, where green waters of the South China Sea meet muddy currents of the Pearl River estuary, a commanding prospect overlooks an important historical sea passage, long ago earning the name Yuan Du Shan, or "hill for ships sailing from afar".

There, in 1729, the seventh year of Yong Shen, authorities of the Ming Dynasty ordered construction of a fort known as Fan Lau, or "Division of the Flows", to form an important link in Lantau's coastal defences against piracy. Alongside its fortifications stood a natural stone column bearing a marked resemblance to a human face and prompting adjacent villagers, whose homes now stand abandoned, to describe the bastion as Shi Shun (Stone Pillar Fort).

The stronghold was placed under the command of the right wing of the Da Pang Battalion. Guarded by forty-eight soldiers and one lieutenant, its main function was to garrison troops mobilized in response to pirate operations in the busy shipping lanes. Rectangular in shape, measuring twenty-one by forty-five metres, it was armed with eight cannons. At one point it was deserted by its troops and briefly occupied by the pirates they had been sent to quell.

In 1900, two years after Lantau Island's inclusion in the New Territories lease, the fort was abandoned, and began to fall into ruin. In 1981 it was declared a monument and nine years later afforded full legal protection under the Antiquities ordinance.

IMPERIAL CUSTOMS TOWER

Junk Bay

In the late nineteenth century, the Chinese Imperial Maritime
Customs Service attempted to ring Hong Kong with customs
stations. The resulting blockade saw stations established on
Cheung Chau and Ma Wan islands, at Sham Shui Po and
Kowloon City.

One such station was established on a bluff at Junk Bay,
overlooking a sweeping panorama of Port Shelter, where a
maze of intricate inlets, skirting Bluff, Sharp and Basalt islands,
offered tempting possibilities for smuggling.

Adjoining the circular lookout tower was a barrack block for
resident personnel who, by the 1890s, were trained in modern
telegraphy, replacing previous methods of communication that
included flag signalling.

The watch tower did not long remain in service. One of
the factors prompting Britain to negotiate the lease of the
New Territories was a desire to remove such impediments to
trade from the immediate environs of the harbour. Once the
lease went into effect in 1898, all Chinese Imperial Maritime
Customs stations were decommissioned.

TANG PAGODA

Ping Shan, Yuen Long

An important feng shui node at Ping Shan, in the north west New Territories, marks the conjunction of dangerous and benevolent force lines meeting at right angles, the former running inland from the sea and the latter descending from the crest of the Castle Peak ridge. Here, in the late fourteenth century, the Tang clan built the "Gathered Stars" pagoda to control the negative and strengthen the positive forces.

Erected six hundred or more years ago, the pagoda was originally seven storeys, alluding to the seven Buddhas said to have existed at different periods. However, it sustained serious damage two hundred years ago that necessitated reconstruction. On the advice of geomancers, it was replaced by the present three-storey structure.

Believed to be especially beneficial to those of the Tang clan with aspirations to scholarship, the pagoda houses, on its top floor, an altar to Fui Shing, the god of examinations. The whole edifice is imbued with wealth and scholarly success. Here the clan gathers for the Ping Shan decennial rituals of Ta Tsiu.

The structure is hexagonal in shape, with each of its three storeys narrower than the one below. It is constructed of local brick and fir poles, the roof having been reinforced. Elaborate corbels divide the floors, each of which bears its own name on a stone tablet at the entrance. The second floor chamber bears the title "Tsui Shing Lau", from which the pagoda as a whole takes its name. Following a fatal fall, the two top floors are generally secured, denying access to drug addicts who stole some of the altar figures.

The Tsui Shing Lau pagoda is the only authentic early pagoda in Hong Kong, and has been recently restored as a monument.

HONG KONG HOUSING AUTHORITY

Verbena Heights, Tseung Kwan O

When its hand was forced by a calamitous fire that destroyed Shek Kip Mei squatter area on Christmas Day 1953, leaving 53,000 destitute, the Hong Kong Government embarked on the world's most ambitious housing programme, providing homes for the maximum number of people in the shortest possible time. Within two decades it became landlord to 1.8 million, representing 42 per cent of the population, and by 1984 that figure had risen to 2.5 million, an increasing share of whom responded to government's offer to sell them the homes they occupied.

The shift from rental accommodation to home ownership became especially marked in the final years of British colonial rule, so that between 1978 and 1997 the government built more than 240,000 subsidised flats for sale under various home ownership schemes. As a result, 52 per cent of the total population now own their homes, compared with 42 per cent just ten years ago.

By the mid seventies it was evident that Hong Kong Island and Kowloon could no longer contain this expansion. To overcome traditional resistance towards relocation anywhere outside the immediate radius of familiar environments, the government announced that most new estates would be sited in the hitherto agricultural hinterland of the New Territories. Anyone wanting to benefit from subsidised accommodation must be prepared to make that psychological leap.

Such tenants became pioneer settlers of mushrooming new towns at Tsuen Wan, Sha Tin, Yuen Long and Tuen Mun, fundamentally altering the nature and appearance of previously pristine farmlands, transforming them into metropolitan areas in their own right. Their homes are a far cry from the primitive H-block layout of Mark I estates, or even of subsequent Marks II to VI, which began pouring off drawing boards faster than improved racing cars off assembly lines. In parallel with the Housing Authority's programmes, the non-profit making Housing Society, established in 1948, has catered for the so-called "sandwich class". Typical of its "flagships" is Anthony Ng's award-winning scheme, Verbena Heights, in Tseung Kwan O.

MARINE POLICE HEADQUARTERS

Tsim Sha Tsui, Kowloon

"None of us want to give her up," said Wally Murison, inspector of building projects. "She's a grand old lady, but she's getting past it. Needs a face-lift." He was describing, at the close of the twentieth century, a building constructed more than a hundred years earlier, the Marine Police Headquarters, perched on a hilltop above Tsim Sha Tsui at the southern extremity of the Kowloon peninsula. Speaking for the police force as a whole, Murison added, "We're all very sentimental about her."

Built in 1884, when the only other development on the peninsula was restricted to military and dockyard installations, the gracious structure was originally two storeys high, commanding the entire sweep of the harbour, where tall-masted tea clippers and naval warships still overshadowed the first steam vessels. Imperially enthusiastic author Rudyard Kipling paints this canvas in his book *From Sea to Sea*: "Beyond the launches lie more steamers than the eye can count and four out of five of these belong to us."

Little was done to renovate the building through its century and more of police service, other than the addition of a third floor in 1920, when modern plumbing was installed, along with ceiling fans. As reminders of a proud tradition, showcases displayed uniforms and regalia. Other memorabilia included the Hotchkiss "noonday" gun, fired from 1947 to 1961, by Jardine Matheson on the Wanchai waterfront, and – as reminders of its role as Japanese Naval Headquarters in World War II – a flag of the rising sun together with Admiral Masaichi's swivel chair. In the grounds stood Hong Kong's only mature date palm, smuggled in by an early botanical enthusiast.

The building was declared an historical monument in 1994, and withdrawal of the police two years later, to a new headquarters at Sai Wan Ho, sparked competition to transform it into a focus for restaurants and shops, an arts centre or museum.

CHI LIN NUNNERY

5 Chi Lin Drive, Diamond Hill

The slow maturity of plans for phased development of the
Chi Lin Nunnery at Diamond Hill allowed for protracted research
of construction methods more than a thousand years old. The only
other structures of its kind still in existence are the Great East Hall
of the Foguang Monastery in Shanxi and the Toshodai-ji in Nara,
one of the most revered buildings in Japan. Both follow architectural
precepts first established in China during the Tang Dynasty.

Earlier phases of the nunnery comprised care and residential
facilities for the elderly, a library of Buddhist texts, a physiotherapy
centre and nun's quarters. But it was the main complex, comprising
sixteen halls, on which has been lavished the greatest care and
attention. Not a single nail, bolt or screw tarnishes structures
whose origins lie as far back as the seventh century AD. But while
contemporary architects appreciate the appearance of the distinctive
Tang style, with its curving "hip" roof, classical proportions and
simple elegance, their understanding of how it was engineered and
assembled remains minimal.

Hundreds of craftsmen were employed in the construction
process, working on the principal components as well as the fine
details, which included tile guards, door knockers, plinths, ceiling
decorations and latticework windows. They toiled not in Hong
Kong but in Anhui, China, where those specialist skills still exist.
The component parts were then shipped to Hong Kong for
assembly on site.

The crowning joy of the nunnery complex is the seven-tiered
Wan Fo Pagoda, symbolizing gradual ascent of the mind to higher
planes and built largely of timber, as are adjoining buildings aligned
along a central axis flanking the main hall. The latter, enshrining
the nunnery's spiritual heart, houses magnificent statues of Buddha.
Other structures, set symmetrically along two sides of a courtyard,
help impart to the whole a balanced, harmonious aspect, instantly
soothing to those who seek solace here from the pressures of one
of Asia's most worldly and frenetic cities.

116

HONG KONG STADIUM

55 Eastern Hospital Road, So Kon Po

Casting around for a site to house a state-of-the-art sports
stadium as its latest gift to the community, The Hong Kong
Jockey Club considered a number of areas throughout
Hong Kong Island and Kowloon, including one pending vacation
by the abysmally ugly Kowloon Walled City, opposite former
Kai Tak international airport. In the end they focused on
redeveloping the existing stadium at So Kon Po, whose capacity
could be increased from twenty-eight thousand to forty thousand
provided consultants worked within the dimensions of the
existing plot.

Architects Hellmuth Obata & Kassebaum assured the club it
could be done, though the tighter fit would entail the loss of an
athletics track around the perimeter of the pitch. To compensate,
the club awarded a grant for a separate facility to house a new
track, and also funded an increased capacity at Aberdeen Stadium
so that children would not lose out on school athletics. Two years
of construction were interrupted only to allow for the staging of
the annual Rugby Sevens and the Viceroy Cup – events sacred to
Hong Kong's sporting calendar.

The launch of this revolutionary new stadium in 1994 unveiled a
showpiece of engineering crowned by scalloped, gossamer-thin
canopies that mask enormous strength and durability in the guise
of a circus tent.

The stadium soon became mired in controversy. Neighbouring
residents complained of high noise levels generated – particularly
during pop concerts – within the oval basin it occupies. The
problem lay in the fact that where the Jockey Club had envisaged
a superb sports stadium, the Urban Council were trying to
manage it as an outdoor amphitheatre, in a location shaped like
a giant natural loudspeaker. Its true vocation remains as the
community's preeminent sports arena, and its greatest success
came when it accommodated a capacity crowd for the Rugby
Sevens World Cup in 1997.

AMBASSADOR HOTEL REDEVELOPMENT

3 Nathan Road, Kowloon

Redevelopment of the former Ambassador Hotel in Nathan Road was nearing completion when the Southeast Asian financial crisis undermined Hong Kong's economy, compelling its watchmaker developers, Stellux, to sell the nearly completed property to its current owners, Oriental Press.

The recession has also hindered the objective of making this prime location the shopping Mecca promised by its imaginative design. This envisaged that the three-level shopping complex, consisting of a triangle and a quadrant connected by bridges would benefit from a free flow of pedestrians between Nathan and Middle roads. While there is no lack of pedestrians passing through, few shop tenants have been found to take advantage of the opportunities they present.

Seen from the southern end of Nathan Road, the main tower looks deceptively cylindrical, but is in fact a semicircular quadrant whose scale is purposely blurred to make it appear bigger and more imposing than its dimensions would otherwise permit. This shape was architect Rocco Yim's response to the presence of the adjacent Sheraton Hotel, which obscures the seaward view from lower floors. Hence the curved façade takes maximum advantage of the view to the southwest, between the Sheraton and Peninsula hotels. Once the building rises above the Sheraton, the semicircular quadrant acquires a conventionally flat façade that exploits the considerably wider panorama of the harbour.

Energy efficiency was another factor dictating this intriguing variation in the building's contours. Subjected to intense sunlight, the convex façade facing west is tiered in segments to minimize its glazing. Horizontal transoms divide each floor into three layers, with only the middle layer serving as window. The flat and sheltered southern face is glazed from floor to ceiling with glass that requires less reflectivity and is therefore more transparent.

TAIKOO PLACE

979 King's Road, Island East

Quarry Bay marine lots one and two became, early in Hong Kong's forays into industrial development, a sugar refinery and shipyard respectively. Today Swire Properties has transformed both beyond recognition into Taikoo Place and Taikoo Shing; the first a complex of office blocks and the second a residential and commercial area with, at its heart, the fast expanding Cityplaza core. Both have come to be recognized as Island East, where the business community, and individual househunters, can seek attractive, viable options to the high rentals of Central District and the congestion of Wanchai and Causeway Bay.

The pride of Island East is Taikoo Place, adjoining the Quarry Bay MTR station and undergoing its second facelift since Swire Properties established the Taikoo Trading Estate here in the mid-seventies. The advent of the MTR's Island Line in the following decade persuaded Swire to switch to sophisticated office accommodation in place of the massive, multi-tier warehouse blocks erected just a few years earlier. The emphasis now is on style, on large areas of air-conditioned public space, on enclosed, elevated walkways punctuated by art exhibits and comfortable seating – in short, on all the felicitous touches that, with few exceptions, other Hong Kong urban centres have overlooked or inadequately supplied.

Commissioned to plan this phased redevelopment, Wong & Ouyang aligned it along Tong Chong (Sugar Mill) Street, connecting new tower blocks, named after English counties, with seamless pedestrian walkways bordered by shops, eateries, tasteful murals and giant sculptures like Two-To-Tango (below). One by one the industrial buildings made way for pristine, curtain-walled towers such as Devon House, Telecom Tower and Dorset House (opposite), linked by a superb glass-enclosed bridge to Lincoln House, where the offices of the South China Morning Post once stood. Catering to executives seeking quality surroundings in which to entertain guests, Swire resurrected the name of a former partner with which it was once allied, in the early China trade days, to create Butterfield's, a private club.

THE LEE GARDENS

111 Leighton Road, Causeway Bay

Three generations of the family dynasty founded by Hysan Lee
have retained possession of much of the original square mile
of land they owned in Causeway Bay. At its hub stood the
Lee Gardens Hotel, for many years the largest in the district and
a distinctive local landmark. Among tenants of its several floors
of office space was the government's Education Department.
In time redevelopment of the immediate environment began to
dwarf the dated building, to the point where a desultory effort
by its long-time patrons failed to save it from demolition.

Architect Dennis Lau was entrusted with the design of its
replacement, in the form of a fifty-storey structure embracing
seventy thousand square metres of office space and twenty
thousand square metres of retail space, but lacking the hotel that
had assured its predecessor a fond niche in the memories of so
many. Lau borrowed two of the themes he had employed in his
much larger design for Central Plaza – a triangular configuration
with blunted corners and a lighting feature that changes colours
over a four-minute cycle.

The tower rises from a much larger podium, leaving a spacious
peninsula four floors high enclosing a circular shopping atrium
crowned by a rooftop restaurant. Cutting through the crest of the
southeastern apex of the triangular tower is a large aperture some
five storeys deep, accommodating a hanging garden for the private
enjoyment of Hysan Lee's successors.

Where once it was overshadowed by structures of later origin in
the crowded Causeway Bay neighbourhood, the Lee Gardens has
now reasserted its pre-eminent position as the tallest on the block.

LEE THEATRE PLAZA

99 Percival Street, Causeway Bay

Childhood memories of watching Chinese opera in the old Lee Theatre shaped an early decision by Dennis Lau to become an architect. His eyes had constantly drifted from the stage performance towards the theatre's baroque dome, across which Apollo raced his flaming chariot. Designed by a French architect in 1920, and completed in 1925, in the days when construction was a slower, more labour-intensive process, the theatre occupied a special niche in Hong Kong's affections, so that its planned demolition in 1991 released a flood of nostalgia and cries of protest.

Several other architects had submitted proposals for redevelopment of the site before the owners invited Lau to offer his ideas. He produced a sketch that won their instant approval because it made clear his intention to preserve as much as possible of the look and style of the original. Commissioned to undertake the design, he and his team carried out painstaking studies of the old theatre before it was reduced to rubble. When the new plaza rose in its place, twenty-two storeys above two basements, it was clear Lau had achieved a striking parallel between the splendour of what was and the glory of what had been.

Too small for anything approaching the Apollo fresco, the cinema incorporated in this structure plays a minor role in a building devoted largely to shops and restaurants, so that Lau concentrated his efforts on the outer fabric and the detailing of the entrance and lobby. He made a particular point of reproducing, as exactly as possible, the peninsula of steps that projected in a triangular configuration from the front of the old building. A popular place of assignation for young lovers meeting before some pending cinema show or theatrical performance, the steps still provide that essential point of rendezvous as just one of the endearing features so faithfully echoed in the new, more vertical alignment of the plaza's façade.

K. WAH CENTRE

191 Java Road, North Point

Simon Kwan & Associates Ltd found inspiration for this twenty-eight-storey office block in a five thousand-year-old Neolithic jade carving. This object, a ritualistic *cong,* is one of man's oldest interpretations of form, comprising a cylinder, representing heaven, enclosed by a cube to symbolize the solidity of earth. Adapting this concept to serve as an architectural structure, Simon Kwan allowed the cylinder to obtrude from the constraints of the cube, enlivening the entire shape of the tower.

To preserve the purity of the whole, he employed uncluttered curtain walling, broken only at two points on the cube's corners and at alternating levels on the curvilinear façades, the object being to emphasize the novelty of the overall edifice as well as to provide garden balconies affording panoramas of Kowloon's hills to the north and Hong Kong Island's to the south. Benefitting from a commanding location on the North Point waterfront, the K. Wah Centre stands as a conspicuous landmark, largely free of neighbouring buildings and reflecting immense slabs and curvatures of sky in tinted glass of a startling bottle-green sheen.

Kwan stresses that the expression of a form so ancient as to be almost spiritual was not his sole consideration. The elemental shape of the *cong,* as a hollow cylinder within a cube, serves admirably as a practical basis for installing a central core of lifts and other utilities, surrounded by open rectangular floor space enclosed by structural pillars pegging its corners and framing the curvilinear bays. What appealed to him most was the opportunity to employ an antique geometry to meet modern requirements, while retaining and reinforcing its timeless beauty.

Because the site once belonged to a shipping company, with rights to its own pier along the harbour frontage, the centre inherited this privilege, of which it takes advantage with direct access to the sea via its own docking facility.

128

ONWARD AND UPWARD

With the passing years, new developments have rapidly succeeded each other, painting in ever larger and more compelling brush strokes on Hong Kong skylines. As if to ensure a measure of durability, in a city forever discontent with its accomplishments, architecture has, at its worst, exchanged grace and form for size and dominance. At its best, it has achieved all of these attributes, with striking contrasts and original innovations that would embellish any urban horizon.

Inured to erosions of their past, to make way for an incessantly pressing and urgent future, the Hong Kong populace lives in a constant air of expectation for what will follow, when the demolition is done and the pile driving begins. They watch as scaffolding takes on form and substance, ascending floor by floor until it transcends its neighbours. They know, if they turn away too long, another part of their city will have altered beyond recognition. For that is the nature of Hong Kong; the price they pay for living in an ever-changing environment that is more a happening than a city; the reward they earn for dwelling among ceaselessly exciting and stimulating surroundings.

In Hong Kong "Watch this space" is more than a teaser for a forthcoming entertainment. It whets the appetite for the way in which the very metropolis is forever refashioning and remodelling itself. It defines the transience of present existence as mere scaffolding for the form and nature of what is to come.